Living under the Smile of God

ROGER C. PALMS

Tyndale House Publishers, Inc.
Wheaton, Illinois

Material taken from *Creation and Fall/Temptation* by Dietrich Bonhoeffer, © 1959 by SCM Press Ltd., used by permission of Macmillan Publishing Co., Inc., New York.

Material taken from *Iron Shoes* by C. Roy Angell, © 1953, 1981, used by permission of Broadman Press, Nashville.

Material taken from *Margaret of Molokai* by Mel White, © 1981, used by permission of Word Books, Waco, Texas.

Material taken from *Prayer Power Unlimited* by J. Oswald Sanders, © 1977, used by permission of Moody Press, Moody Bible Institute of Chicago.

Material taken from *Studies in the Sermon on the Mount,* Vol. 2, by D. Martin Lloyd-Jones, used by permission of William B. Eerdmans Publishing Company, Grand Rapids.

Material taken from *Thoughts on Christian Sanctity* by H. C. Moule, used by permission of Moody Press, Moody Bible Institute of Chicago.

Material taken from *True Spirituality* by Francis A. Schaeffer, © 1971, used by permission of Tyndale House Publishers, Inc., Wheaton, Illinois.

Second printing, July 1984
Library of Congress Catalog Card Number 83-50969
ISBN 0-8423-2489-5, cloth
ISBN 0-8423-2490-9, paper
Copyright © 1984 by Roger C. Palms

CONTENTS

ONE
I Don't See God Smiling
7

TWO
When You Want to Be Honest with God
19

THREE
Praying When Prayer Doesn't Seem to Work
31

FOUR
In the Joy of Ascending Moments
43

FIVE
Becoming Free
57

SIX
When People Don't Like You
73

SEVEN
When I Am Pressured to Do What Is Wrong
85

EIGHT
As God Goes to Work with Me
99

NINE
With Family Love Around You
111

TEN
Growing When You Are All Alone
123

ELEVEN
If I Should Die Before I Wake
133

TWELVE
Enjoying the Smile of God
147

O N E
I Don't See God Smiling

He was four years old when he died. He was a happy boy singing a Sunday school song. The car skidded and crashed. As his mother bent down to him, he said, "Mommy, I'm going to see Jesus now."

Where is God?

A middle-aged woman is bitter. All she's ever wanted from God is to be a wife and mother, to do the domestic things that go with being a housewife.

After high school she took an ordinary, unchallenging job. It was to be only temporary. She really wanted to get married. Through the years she waited, occasionally changing to other "temporary" jobs, always anticipating the day when she'd be able to have a husband, make a home, and build a family.

She was counseled to develop a career, attend college, and plan for her own future. But no. She knew what she wanted.

She talked to God about it—often. "Surely God knows I would be a dedicated wife, a committed mother," she'd say. "Surely I'm better suited than many women who aren't excited about their marriages or their children. Why does God give others what I want? Why doesn't God satisfy me? Why isn't God smiling at me?"

Where is God?

How can you answer the question of the man who, one week before he is to begin his eagerly awaited retirement, learns that he has cancer? What can you say to the mother whose baby is born with Down's syndrome? What comfort can be given to the father and mother whose student son writes them a note, saying, "I can't make it," and slashes his wrists?

These aren't evil people. They haven't rejected God. These are people who look for, even wish for, the smile of God. But they don't see it. These stories can be multiplied; you know others.

Where is God?

Sometimes when we talk about the smile of God it's only a humorous comment. "God isn't smiling at me," we say.

One morning I was driving along comfortably on the freeway in my Volkswagen when suddenly a tire on a car ahead of me came loose. It bounced back, was knocked down by another car, and before I could stop or swerve I drove up on top of it, pulling the tire along until the car came grinding to a stop with all four wheels of my Volkswagen off the ground.

There I sat, traffic piling up behind me, drivers in the other two lanes laughing at me as they zoomed by. Eventually enough people gathered to lift the car off the tire and I drove on, embarrassed.

When I got home that night, seeking sympathy for my suffering, I told my wife about the embarrassing event. She started laughing. When she finally got enough control of herself to speak, she said, "Why didn't you just sit there? It might have hatched!"

God wasn't smiling at me that day.

Well, that incident was embarrassing, but not serious. It's when everything crumbles around us that we begin to wonder about God.

This week, as I was writing this, two of my friends lost their sons. Both of these young men were in their early twenties. One had just made a public commitment in a church service: "Lord, I'll go where you want me to go." Within a few days he was gone, home with God.

Is God smiling when people lose their young sons? Afterward, these parents echoed the thought in Romans 8: "Yes, I believe that all things do work together for good to them that love God, to them who are the called according to his purpose." And by the time of the funerals, friends were saying it too.

That's hard for some people to accept. But go through that with a committed Christian and you see something of that dimension that is not make believe. It is real. They know.

Good does come, even in great suffering, to those who live under the smile of God. But some people miss it. The legalist misses it because he has become cold and formal, building his faith on God's revelation as an abstract thing. The teachings of God have become historical, objective, impersonal. They become carved in stone, laws to be obeyed with a strictness that eliminates the joy of life in Christ. The legalist misses the smile of God.

So does the existentialist, but for a different reason. Because he is so caught up with his own experiences, he thinks God is what he feels God is. He thinks he has God's truth when all he has are that moment's feelings about God's truth. The sensations of the moment are his teachers and he cannot build anything stable on them. They change, they fluctuate. He too misses the smile of God.

Many evangelical Christians talk about the smile of God, but don't experience it. That's because, unfortunately, they have been led along a rosy path of belief that makes them think they must always see God smiling. Our God, some persons are led to believe, would not allow anything bad to happen to us.

But if we persist in this wishful thinking, in our desire for the smooth life, we will miss the joy of the companionship of the One who will walk with us even through the valley of the shadow of death. We will miss the depth, the height, and the breadth of God.

We have mistaken our comfort for his companionship.

D. Martyn Lloyd-Jones said: "I once heard a man use a phrase which affected me very deeply at the time, and still does. I am not sure it is not one of the most searching statements I have ever heard. He said that the trouble with many of us Christians is that we believe on the Lord Jesus Christ, but that we do not believe Him."

He has called us to believe him and to live out that belief. It is a lie to tell people that good fortune always belongs to those who have faith. It is a lie because we are still in the fallen world and subject to it. We hurt people, heap guilt upon them, contribute to their pain in a cruel way when we insist that any problems in their lives are their own fault, the result of lacking faith. Our faith is in the "man of sorrows, and acquainted with grief" (Isa. 53:3, KJV) who will go through sorrows and grief with us. He knows, the Son of God knows; God proved his smile in Jesus Christ.

We turn in faith to God as one ready to receive, as flowers to the sun, as children to their parents—and we don't presume to determine the meaning of the events of our lives, no matter what they are. Meaning is determined by the thinking of God.

Scripture tells me that God is thinking about me all the time. That's hard to grasp, but it's true. "And when I waken in the morning, you are still thinking of me" (Ps. 139:18, TLB).

God said, " 'For I know the plans that I have for you,' declares the Lord, 'plans for welfare and not for calamity to give you a future and a hope. Then you will call upon Me and come and pray to Me, and I will listen to you. And you will seek Me and find Me, when you search for Me with all your heart. And I will be found by you, and I will restore your fortunes' " (Jer. 29:11-14, NASB). God means that!

Does God have good plans for me? Yes, he does. Are his plans for my good, my welfare? Yes, they are —he says so. Does he want to give me a future and a hope? Yes, he promises that. Can I call upon him? Pray to him? Will he hear me? Yes, he has already promised that. He said he would, and he will never go back on his Word.

But there is a part, something else, that depends upon each of us. Notice: "You will seek Me and find Me, when you search for Me with all your heart." When all your heart—not part of your heart, all—is involved in the search for God, you will find him. " 'And I will be found by you,' declares the Lord." There is no question about that.

God is smiling whether or not I sense that smile. The trees in the forest are there whether or not I am near the forest. The stars in the sky are there whether my eyes are open or closed. The sun is there whether or not the clouds block it out. The reality of God's smile has nothing to do with our seeing that smile. I have to come to know that, to trust in the smile of God.

It was difficult for me to learn that. Not long ago, I experienced slander to the point that it is still painful to think about. I had contributed an article to a Christian journal on the subject of the clergy and their families. It contained both negative and positive examples put in to encourage clergy to spend more time with their families. The editor of that journal, without my knowledge or consent, deleted the most positive examples of family togetherness, leaving mostly negative examples, and then added in the first person—as if I had said it myself—a statement that implied I had family problems and had left the ministry because of it. When the magazine was published and I read those words, the shock overwhelmed me. The magazine had published a lie about the most important parts of my life—my family and my ministry. I thought of all my colleagues in ministry, my friends, my relatives, the people I had served in churches. What would they think? My reputation as a family man and a minister of the gospel was soiled by what an editor wanted that article to say.

We all know people who claim to have been misquoted, and often we suspect, "Well, there must have been something to it or it wouldn't have been published." We assume the worst. When something is in print, we tend to believe it.

As I talked to friends (and some admitted they had read the article but hadn't wanted to say anything about it because they assumed the quote was true), I had advice ranging from "sue them," to "forget it." I feel that a lawsuit only succeeds in pitting one Christian against another and doesn't eliminate the wrong anyway. Once printed, the damage was done. But could I turn the other cheek? Isn't something that damages a person's reputation worse than a slap in the face?

I had to go back to God and ask him, "Why? Where were you in all of this? Didn't you know what was going on? Couldn't you have stopped it?"

In the months that followed I learned at least three things through that experience. First, I learned that I am not God. I do not stand outside creation. I am within creation and the Fall and I am subject to all of its weaknesses and evil, including the actions of other people.

Secondly, I learned that my "reputation," the protection of my "good name," can become sin to me if it becomes a point of merit or prestige to be valued in itself. In myself I have no good name. The only good name I have is "Christian," and I cannot worship that; I must worship him whose name I claim. I must live the name "Christian"; I must live a good reputation because I live it in Christ. My reputation is not mine for my own sake; my reputation is that of a "Christ one" to be honored for his sake.

Third, I learned that just as the Master was himself

subjected to slander ("They say, Behold a man glut-tonous, and a friend of publicans and sinners"[Matt. 11:19, KJV]), so I am subject to slander and all that it brings upon a person. This world can destroy a per-son's reputation. This world does cause suffering. I learned that I am not above my Master, and if in a small way I too am momentarily a "man of sorrows, and acquainted with grief" (Isa. 53:3, KJV) when I am neither purity nor goodness as he was, what must he have suffered having known all of God—in purity, goodness, and grace?

There is probably a fourth lesson in all of this, and I think I am learning it. That lesson is this: there will always be slander, hurt, physical disease, emotional stress, and spiritual struggle for me as long as I am on this earth. I'm not finished with all of it yet; there will be more. That is a reason to long for heaven. Were this life so good, so blessed, all of the time—though it is good some of the time—I would come to like it too much. I might even come to love it. But there is al-ways a reminder—both in the things that happen to me and in what I see happening to those around me—that I am heading for a better place. This is not an escape mentality but a reasonable and pleasant antici-pation. Heaven will soon be mine.

Francis Schaeffer is right when he says, "When I am dead both to good and bad, I have my face turned towards God."

I did not get these answers from God right at the time I was feeling the pain of that published article; I merely suffered and endured it then. But weeks later these answers came as I thought about our Lord and read about other Christians in our church history who were maligned and misunderstood. A wise pastor, with many years of experience, explained to me that those who have watched me over the years will not believe what they read. He told me that I should just continue to live my life before the Lord—and trust him with what happened, and I have vowed to do that.

Then God began to deal with me in an even deeper way. I read these words by Francis Schaeffer in *True Spirituality:* "Every time I see something right in another man, it tends to minimize me, and it makes it easier for me to have a proper creature-creature relationship. But each time I see something wrong in others, it is dangerous, for it can exalt self, and when this happens, my open fellowship with God falls to the ground. So when I am right, I can be wrong. In the midst of being right, if self is exalted, my fellowship with God can be destroyed."

I thought about my attitude toward people who write material that slanders, and I thought about forgiveness. The early church practiced the love that Jesus taught. It was a mark of the Christian community. It is true that slander, intended or not, is not love. Destructive words are not printed in love. The injury of another person is no light thing. But forgiveness is even more important. It was a lesson that I had to learn.

I also decided that when I hear something or read something about others, I must not be too quick to believe it, for I know now that it may not be true. I learned something else, the comfort that comes from the awareness that God knows everything that happens to me. It is true that not even a sparrow falls to the ground without God knowing about it.

I am worth far more than a sparrow. I belong to the One who also suffered without cause, he the perfect sinless one—a claim I could never make for myself. And I had to ask myself, since Jesus was faithful can I as his follower be less? I know that I cannot live a wholesome life if I harbor anger or resentment. I cannot serve God that way. I will forfeit my privilege to live under the loving smile of God.

Whatever the world brings to us, we are still his. And that means far more than a pleasant life, a good reputation, personal worth, private and family success, or even a happy state of mind. For there is more to living than just the living of life, more to life than life itself. And I believe now more than ever that a Christian does live under the smile of God, for in a bad situation I saw how God turned my thoughts toward him, and I learned something deeper about his love as he tenderly taught me something deeper about myself.

Scripture tells us: "Dear friends, do not be surprised at the painful trial you are suffering, as though something strange were happening to you. But rejoice that you participate in the sufferings of Christ, so that you may be overjoyed when his glory is revealed. If you are insulted because of Christ, you are blessed, for the spirit of glory and of God rests on you. If you suffer, it should not be as a murderer or thief or any other kind of criminal, or even as a meddler. However, if you suffer as a Christian, do not be ashamed, but praise God that you bear that name. For it is time for judgment to begin with the family of God; and if it begins with us, what will the outcome be for those who do not obey the gospel of God? And 'If it is hard for the righteous to be saved, what will become of the ungodly and the sinner?' So then, those who suffer according to God's will should commit themselves to their faithful Creator and continue to do good" (1 Pet. 4:12-19, NIV).

But maybe you know deep down inside that you have strayed from God and that is the problem. You don't sense God's smile because you have purposely turned away from him—your back is turned to God. It happens. Remember Uzziah? Those Old Testament individuals like Uzziah are good for us to study. They are a warning for us not to do the same thing.

Uzziah, the Bible says (2 Chron. 26), worshiped God steadily—at first. "He set himself to seek God." What a beautiful description of a man. "He was marvelously helped, till he was strong." But then look what happened: "But when he was strong he grew proud." He became bold with God's gift of power; he tried to usurp the rights that were not his. God struck him with leprosy. And when he died, people didn't say, "There was a man who 'set himself to seek God.'" Instead they said, "He is a leper." He had left God, left the strength, and was remembered no more for what he once was. If only he had heeded the warnings and turned back. If only . . . .

Your own sorrow, your own remorse, may be your blatant rebellion against God, and it tells you God is not smiling. You feel it. What can you do? God himself gives the answer. The Bible says, "Yet the Lord pleads with you still: Ask where the good road is, the godly paths you used to walk in, in the days of long ago. Travel there, and you will find rest for your souls" (Jer. 6:16, TLB).

God wants to support you strongly. You don't have to go on frantically looking for God. God is looking for you to support you with his strength. Give your heart back to him.

David, in spite of his evil before God, in spite of taking another man's wife and then killing that man, turned back to God. You are no worse than David. Take the way back that he took. He prayed, "Create in me a clean heart, O God; and renew a right spirit within me" (Ps. 51:10, KJV).

That is still the way back. "God opposes the proud but gives grace to the humble. Humble yourselves, therefore, under God's mighty hand, that he may lift you up in due time" (1 Pet. 5:5, 6, NIV).

That is now, and always will be, the way to come back and live "under the smile of God."

T W O
When You Want
to Be Honest with God

It was two o'clock in the morning. I was asleep in my hotel room when suddenly behind my head came the pounding of rock music over a stereo system that vibrated the wall. It continued for an hour while I lay there angrily fuming as my head started pounding.

The next night it happened again, and the next. I had no choice. If I were going to get a night's sleep, I had to move.

Unless the hotel manager said something, whoever was playing the music night after night probably still doesn't know the headaches he gave me, or the trouble I went through packing and moving. But that experience made me do some serious thinking about myself.

Do I too annoy people without even realizing that I am doing it? I know what others do that annoys me, but what about things that I do? Are people quietly fuming because I've irritated them somehow? Can I be sure at the beginning of a day that I will not hurt anybody, and at the close of the day can I know for certain that I didn't? Can I know that wherever I have gone there has come encouragement and a building-up, that I have brought pleasure and peace?

I went to my Bible; I needed a checklist. I needed to

find out about me. I learned that "wise men turn away wrath" (Prov. 29:8, KJV). If that is true, and God's Word says it is, then the opposite must also be true—that one who doesn't pay attention to the wisdom that comes from God brings wrath.

I found the words of Jesus: "A good man out of the good treasure of his heart bringeth forth that which is good; and an evil man out of the evil treasure of his heart bringeth forth that which is evil" (Luke 6:45, KJV). My actions, then, are determined by what is in my heart. I don't need to check what I *do* so much as I need to check my heart.

And when I went on to read Ecclesiastes, I found, "For God shall bring every work into judgment" (Eccles. 12:14, KJV). He sees everything and he will judge everything. God wants to bring good treasure out of our hearts because he is the judge of the treasure. He wants to have a good word for us at the Judgment; he wants to be able to say to us, "Well done, thou good and faithful servant: . . . enter thou into the joy of thy lord" (Matt. 25:21, KJV).

And I found even more hope in my search of the Word. In Micah I learned that even when I fall and "bear the indignation of the Lord, because I have sinned against him . . . he will bring me forth to the light" (Mic. 7:9, KJV). He will because he promised.

I can relax in him; when I slip I can know that he will bring me to the light again. I don't have to live in the fear that I will offend and be condemned for it. God in his love and through his Word has offered the guidelines to keep me from hurting others, even unknowingly.

My rock music neighbor in that hotel helped me to make that discovery. I'm certain God knew that he would. He is a loving Father; he doesn't miss opportunities like that.

More than once I have found myself saying to people in a counseling situation: "No, life isn't fair. Where did you get the idea that it was?" We have all asked, "Why do the wicked prosper?" And we have stood silently with those who know tragedy and pain as they ask, with tears streaming down their faces, "Where is God?" Life isn't fair!

Life, in fact, is a tragedy. We should know that. The Bible is quite explicit about man's fall. We are not what God intended us to be nor are we living in the kind of world God intended. We are fallen creatures in a fallen world. We are victims of broken relationships, of a fallen structure where there is disease, decay, anger, hate, war, strife, misery. We live in that world. We are not yet in heaven. Though we have been redeemed and brought close to the One who gives peace in the midst of struggle and healing in the course of pain, we are still in this world—a painful and tragic world.

But there is nothing wrong with being honest with God about what we are enduring and how we feel about it. It is not wrong for me to feel like pounding my fists against God and saying, "This is not fair!" There is nothing wrong with saying, "Why did you let this happen to me?" No, there is nothing wrong with that if we know to whom we are speaking and can come to the point of saying, as Job did, "Though he slay me, yet will I trust in him" (Job 13:15, KJV).

I like Job. He is my kind of man. I like him because he is honest. He respected, trusted, and honored God but he wasn't afraid to ask "Why?"

His friends, those counselors with easy words, were not evil men. Job admitted that what they taught about sin was true. "Who knoweth not such things as these" (Job 12:3, KJV). He didn't dispute it. But he came right back and protested his innocence in all his suffering and his helplessness in not being able to confront God about it. "Oh, how I long to speak directly to the Almighty. I want to talk this over with God himself" (Job 14:6, TLB). Then with true honesty in his pain, he cried out, "Give . . . a little rest, won't you?" (Job 14:6, TLB), and "Don't abandon me" (Job 13:21, TLB). Job was an honest man.

Though we can show our human feelings, and they are not to be denied, God is—and always will be—Lord. God made us; he gave us all that we are. He may stand by while all we count dear is taken away. But we have no argument. God is God.

Yet we are not victims; we are his. It is the lost, the separated ones, those who deny God who must always be uncertain, always feeling like victims of the toss of the coin. That is not the stand for us who believe in God, who have transferred our trust from ourselves to the Lord Jesus Christ.

There is suffering for us and there always will be so long as we live on this earth. God knows that. There is no need to pretend otherwise. It is not somehow more spiritual to lie about our hurts as if God didn't know the truth. Nor do we always have to say in a Pollyannaish way that good will come of it. There is sometimes a reward to suffering, but not always.

22

We try to look for the teaching, the good, the blessing. Often we can find it in the grief of life. But it is not always so. Some events have no reason to them so far as we can see, no teaching value, nothing —just pain. Sometimes suffering isn't rewarding in any way. Sometimes it's sterile. Sometimes there is nothing in it. Sometimes there is no reason for it, no purpose, no apparent good coming from it. All we can do is face it.

But we can still meet God in those sterile times in the same way that we meet him in any other situation or event. He does not desert us in the suffering or the illness, the pain or the mental torture. He is as close as he always was. No. Rather, in our emptiness, in our suffering, we draw closer to him. We hold on—not for more money, or power, not even a "blessing"— we just hold on to God. That is the only answer for much of what hurts.

Whereas before we may not have felt this desire for him, now in pain we have that need for him, and it is a desperate need. Now we turn to him. Now we want to take God's hand.

The void of the difficult moment clears everything between him and ourselves, and we stand with our empty cup asking for it to be filled. Before, we may have tried to fill that cup ourselves, with our wisdom, our strength, our skills, our abilities. Not now. Now in the pain and the emptiness we admit we have nothing, and we say in our nothingness, "Fill my cup, Lord." And he does. He gives us enough. He brings us through. Then, quietly, we breathe our anguished, "Thank you." We have found him close.

If God can offer so much in our emptiness and pain,

what can he offer in our times of plenty?

Haggai knew. Haggai was preparing the people to build the house of God. The people were living in their own paneled houses and thought they had so much. Actually, they didn't have much at all. "Ye have sown much, and bring in little; ye drink, but ye are not filled with drink; ye clothe you, but there is none warm; and he that earneth wages earneth wages to put it into a bag with holes" (Hag. 1:6, KJV).

We don't have much either, even when we think we do. Maybe in our honesty we need to be aware that we are building our own little temples and are ignoring God. God has a building that he wants to build, a spiritual temple. Maybe honesty requires that we look around at our other temples and admit: "All that I have isn't anything after all," and ask him to build and fill his temple in us. Honesty demands openness—about ourselves, about him, about where we are. Honesty doesn't pretend.

It is the mark of friendship to tell the truth. If you are God's friend, if you walk with him, if you have known him in the good times and were honest with him then, be honest with him in the bad times too. Don't be afraid to say what you feel. That's being honest.

Of course, some won't do that. They avoid God, ignore him; their resentment or anger continues, festering. "God is not God," they say. "He can't be a God of love," they insist. There have always been people like that. Some have even been our teachers. Harold K. Walker comments that the philosopher Jean-Paul Sartre was like that, and his reaction to God was, in reality, a reaction against himself. "One who reads Sartre's biography is constrained to feel that his existentialism, so devoid of spiritual depth and with scorn for the very idea of God, is primarily the consequence not of rational thought, but of self-hate bottled within him. Hate for himself and for those who nurtured him left him unable to believe that love is anything but phony. Of course, the God who is love is phony too."

Honesty is not only an expression to God about the feelings we have for him but an awareness of ourselves. We have to admit what we feel and we have to admit what we are. There is sin, there is guilt, and we are loaded with both. Denying this is like denying the diagnosis of cancer—it is still there. Shutting our eyes won't make it go away. David A. Redding said: "Making guilt inadmissable has made it all the more dangerous. Since it is undefined, sin now enjoys a reign of terror. We refuse to believe that there is anything to forgive. We will not recognize an occasion for a Redeemer."

David said in Psalm 119:176: "I have gone astray like a lost sheep; seek thy servant" (KJV). That is what Isaiah was also telling us: "All we like sheep have gone astray" (Isa. 53:6, KJV).

Jesus describes us as sheep without a shepherd. David had enough experience as a shepherd to know that sheep get lost easily. David was a smart man; he knew he was like a sheep, prone to wander off. Other people are lost too, but are not smart enough to know it. They are the ones who haven't yet said, "Seek thy servant." We have a need for God to come looking for us.

Being honest with God in personal pain or individual despair is not an experience we should go through on our own. We need perspective, we need the help and vision of others. "Is any sick among you? let him call for the elders of the church; and let them pray over him, anointing him with oil in the name of the Lord" (James 5:14, KJV).

Paul served God and suffered for God—but not alone. He had support; his letters show it. Josiah Royce pointed out: "Mystical piety can never either exhaust or express the whole Christian doctrine of life. For the Christian doctrine of life, in its manifoldness, in the intensity and variety of the human interests to which it appeals, is an essentially social doctrine. Private individual devotion can never justly interpret it.

"Paul was a mystic; but he was a mystic with a community to furnish the garden where the mystical flowers grew; and where the fruits of the spirit were ripened, and where all the gifts of the spirit found their only worthy expression."

When we speak to God about our feelings, our angers, our hurts, we need the help of Christian friends; we need them to keep us straight lest we are guided only by our own emotions.

We are not, in the light of the holiness of God, ever justified to question him as if we are equals. Job knew that. But we are, in our humanity, allowed to express our honest feelings to him. Still, as we do that, even though we may be corrected by our brethren, we can also look for and expect their empathy. We can look for an arm around the shoulder, a tender touch, an embrace, assurance, the words, "I understand." Their tears blend with ours. We draw from their love; and through it we can know the quality of oneness, the bearing of one another's burdens, for that's what Scripture urges lest those burdens become so heavy they break our backs.

We need the help of other believers, and they need ours. But we don't need their condemnation and they don't need ours either. We have a right to stand before God to be judged; they do too. And we all will be. But only God is God. The wood, hay, and stubble in our lives is his to burn away. We have a right to be corrected by loving brethren and sometimes the right to correct them, but we don't have to take the cynical judgment of people who are quick to see our sins but not their own, the sliver in our eye but not the railroad tie in theirs.

Often I meet people who are truly done in—not so much by their sin, though that is overwhelming, but by the destructive accusations of another Christian. We cannot judge another because we have not been there with them. We cannot because we are not allowed to. "Judge not, that ye be not judged" (Matt. 7:1, KJV) We can only be silent and care, counsel as asked, and gently correct when needed—not out of our superiority but out of an awareness of our own sin.

When one is crying out to God we can stand with him, hold him, help him, and let him cry. He is a friend of God; God will hear his friend. Maybe he is a wayward friend, but his anger, his anguish, his tears, his cries, are the reality of a soul wanting God again— and that's good.

But honesty does not always mean anger with God. Sometimes honesty brings us to the confession that we doubt him. Who has not at least once in his life doubted God? We can have one glorious experience after another, experiences of God answering prayer, experiences with his guidance, experiences even with his comfort; yet, because we are so human, the next time we go to prayer we doubt that he will answer.

Everyone has been through that or will sometime. But we have a great example of our own humanity in action and how to handle it in the story of the prophet Elijah. Look at this man of God. In chapter 18 of 1 Kings, he experienced the power of prayer as he called upon God before the prophets of Baal, and fire from heaven came down on the water-soaked sacrifice and consumed it. The Baal worshippers had to declare, "The Lord, he is the God" (1 Kings 18:39, KJV). Right then Elijah had dramatic evidence of God answering prayer.

And later, in quiet faith, Elijah could see a great rainstorm coming—even when there were no clouds in the sky. He knew what God could do. He was confident, and God brought the rain.

Yet on another day this same Elijah, now depressed and uncertain, stood on the mountain with his mantle covering his face, seeking visible evidence of the presence of God passing by.

God said to him: "What are you doing here, Elijah?" In other words, "Where is your faith, man? What are you doing, hiding in this cave with your scarf over your face?" Because it was this Elijah who, having seen the power of God, having experienced dramatic answers to prayer, was still scared by the threat of Jezebel. She sent a messenger to Elijah telling him that he was going to die. And in 1 Kings 19, Elijah's humanity shows. He was afraid and ran for his life. Crawling under a juniper tree, he cried out to God.

God met Elijah that day, but not in the wind, not in the earthquake, not in the fire, but in a still, small voice.

This was the mighty man of God, scared by the verbal threats of a Jezebel. He couldn't handle the threat. This is the man who had seen more of God's strength than most human beings have ever seen. But this day God had to send an angel to help him. Elijah had to experience the drama of an angel giving him cakes baked on a hot stone and a drink of water to believe in the help of God.

Experience told Elijah he could trust God; reason told him he could trust God. But his human frailties made him afraid. His doubts still won out.

We are like that; we know we are. And, like the father of the boy whom Jesus healed, we can only say, "Lord, I believe; help thou mine unbelief" (Mark 9:24, KJV). Because no matter the number of experiences we have with the power of God, we will still doubt again. Knowing that gives us an honesty when we turn to God on our knees and say, "Oh, God, help me!"

"Let me sense your smile."

That's honesty, and that's good.

THREE
Praying When Prayer
Doesn't Seem to Work

One Saturday in Houston, Texas, I toured the National Aeronautics and Space Administration (NASA). It was the same week that the second space shuttle, Columbia, was launched. I left the main tourist attractions and, escorted by a project engineer, climbed into the simulator, the practice unit of Columbia. It was an exact duplicate of the one that went into space.

As I sat in the commander's seat, I tried to imagine what it must be like to be in space. But even as I pretended, I knew that in reality, "I'm on the ground." I will probably never get off the ground in Columbia or in any other spacecraft. I can only guess what it might be like in space. I am earthbound; that is my reference point.

But others know what it is like not to have Earth as a reference point. Once in space astronauts think about a particular focus. They have to be strapped in someplace, or they float adrift. They wear suction cups on their feet to enable them to stand. These suction cups release with a twist of the foot, then hold firm again with the proper placement. Astronauts need to be attached somewhere in order to work. If they aren't, they can't even push a switch on a computer, for in trying to push switches they push themselves backward. That's a problem with weightlessness.

And when they sleep, it doesn't matter whether they sleep on the "top" of the bunk or on the opposite side of it, the "bottom" of the bunk, or even sleep standing up. There is no "top" or "bottom," no "up" or "down" in space. They shut their eyes and their inner reference tells them that they are lying down. Since there is no weight, it doesn't matter which way they are facing when they sleep—up, down, or sideways. Sleep comes because their minds decide for them which way is up and which way is down.

We are in a weightless world too. There are no fixed reference points, no "up" or "down," no right way or wrong way. The only reference we have is in the mind of each person—he decides his reference point. He decides to what he will be tied; he determines each step he takes. Without a reference point he isn't able to function. He can't accomplish anything.

In a society without fixed points we have to decide to make our own or we will be adrift and every action will have a counterthrust to it.

People have to be committed, but only those who determine that they will be, who have a reference point, will ever touch the world in a meaningful way. The Christian, with reference to the Rock and obedience to the high calling of God in Christ Jesus, has a reason for commitment. Why? Because he doesn't "want out."

God's Word says: "Thou wilt keep him in perfect peace, whose mind is stayed on thee" (Isa. 26:3, KJV). We are urged to be "transformed by the renewing of [our] mind, that [we] may prove what *is* that good, and acceptable, and perfect, will of God" (Rom. 12:2,

KJV). We are told, "Let this mind be in you, which was also in Christ Jesus" (Phil. 2:5, KJV).

Astronauts train their minds and fix a reference point even when they go to sleep; it is the only way they can live in their weightless environment. Christians do that too, all the time, in this "weightless" environment in which we live. For there are no fixed social values for us anymore, and if we function like the rest of society we will drift too. And with no fixed position, no matter what we do, no matter what we try to touch in life, it will push us as much as we try to push against it. We will be useless.

In our daily existence only obedience to the guidance that God gives will keep us going; only commitment to him will keep us from floating. We will walk only when we clamp down on him—he alone is firm; he is unchanging. We stand or move in what is fixed—God—and we know that if we move from that point of reference we will start to drift again.

With God, your reference point spiritually is always relational, not existential. Check this again and again, not for the sake of having sensations or voices coming to you from the outside but simply to know how you are doing. That is what prayer is, a relational conversation with our reference point. God is our focus, and because he is, we can act.

Prayer isn't something that "delivers." Prayer isn't a computer, a button we push. Prayer is a relationship with God. Prayer is listening; prayer is talking. Prayer is moving along in the confidence that God is guiding whether or not we happen to be aware of where we are at the moment. What we are certain of is that no matter where we are, he is there too.

A baby cries when he doesn't see his mother. She has to show herself and say, "Here I am. Mommy's right here," and then he is at peace. As the child grows older he still needs mother, but it's enough to know that mother is in the next room. He knows to whom he belongs. And though some think they "grow up" and don't need to be looked after or need God, they are only kidding themselves. Their inability to cope is proof enough of their need for God. Our maturity in praying is a constant renewing of our reference contact. God is there, near us, whether or not we always see evidence of him.

God isn't always saying to us, "Here I am." He doesn't have to. We don't keep track of him; he is keeping track of us. Thomas à Kempis said, "My son, trust not the emotion of the moment; for whatsoever it may be, it will soon give place to another. As long as thou livest in this world, thou art subject to change, even against thy will. Thus thou art now glad, now sad; now diligent, now listless; now grave, now light-hearted. But he that is wise and well-instructed in the things of the spirit standeth above these changing emotions. He is not swayed by personal feelings, nor doth he study from which quarter the wind of instability bloweth; but only that his whole mind and intention are directed to the right and wished-for end. Thus will he be able to remain steadfast and unshaken in the midst of many changes; for that his singleness of purpose is directed unceasingly to Me."

Satan would like to have us measure God's concern for us only by what God shows in a tangible way. If he can get a person to think about measurable results, visible answers, physical gifts, then the moment we don't see them he can hint, then suggest, then boldly declare, "Prayer doesn't work." He will have been successful in the oldest deception. He will have changed our reference point.

God is our reference point because we have determined that, for us, he will live in our hearts; we will be his person—heart, soul, mind, and strength. That's a trust act. This is "up," we say—and we rest in that. How do we know it is "up"? Because the One who lives in us knows. We are concentrating on him, deriving our balance, our focus, our direction, our ability to act from him.

God should be our focus, not the act of praying. Prayer doesn't have to "work." God answers prayer because he is God, not because we have to see answers. Don't get confused about that. Too many people teach that prayer is a form of magic, and their belief comes very close to the occult. Satan is subtle; he knows what he is doing when he turns people from God who *is* to prayer as something that works.

The efficacy of prayer does not depend upon my ability as "pray-er" or on the intensity of my praying. It does depend upon my trust. But even that trust, that faith, is not strictly my own doing. "It is the gift of God: not of works, lest any man should boast" (Eph. 2:8, 9, KJV). Faith is the work of the Holy Spirit. The efficacy of my prayer is based on my desire to have the Divine Intercessor be my intercessor. "There is one God, and one mediator between God and men, the man Christ Jesus" (1 Tim. 2:5, KJV). We have Jesus standing in the place of prayer on our behalf. He is the one who understands us, our circumstances, our world, and who knows how to intercede for us because he knows us and he knows the Father.

We cannot go along on our feelings, or by what we think we know, or what we have conjectured in our own minds. For then we will have made for ourselves a god who is no bigger than we are. The Son knows the Father, and he is our High Priest, our Intercessor, our Go-between, the One who has entered the Holy of Holies on our behalf.

The question, therefore, is not, "Does prayer work for me?" but rather, "Is my relationship to God the Son as it ought to be?" Am I concentrating on that work of obedience that places me under the command and control of the Savior? Through his lordship, he is interceding on my behalf. God answers prayer for my sake because it is first of all for Jesus' sake. I am his and he lives in me. He cares about that which is his own, and I am his own. I know it on the basis of his promise and finished work.

Dietrich Bonhoeffer talks about God being aware of the Son, Christ Jesus. My Intercessor is neither overwhelmed by nor limited by my limitations or by that which overwhelms me. God hears me praying because God hears his Son praying. And if indeed the relationship is as it should be, a vine-and-branches relationship, then we can cling to and live in the freedom of John 15:7: "If ye abide in me, and my words abide in you, ye shall ask what ye will, and it shall be done unto you" (KJV).

Prayer "works" because we can daily abide in the One who is the Intercessor, the One who is the High Priest, the One who is Lord. We are his, not because we think so or feel so, but because it *is* so on the basis of his great redemptive transaction for us. Through the cross and the resurrection, he is there on my behalf.

And even if disaster comes, realize that he has you; thank him for his leading because he is leading you even if you can't see it immediately.

We pray, and we may think no answer comes. But we keep on going in trust because he doesn't have to give us every answer. He is God; that is enough. He repeats in his Word that he is near. That's what we believe in—his promise, not our definition of results. When we are dealing with the omnipotent God, the word "result" is a puny word. God is much, much bigger than just what we want. God is big enough to want for us what he wants. He comes to us in his timing, with his acts, by his will. Our act is the faith act.

J. Oswald Sanders said, "For our encouragement, we should remember that the walls of Jericho did not fall until the Israelites had circled them a full thirteen times and then shouted the shout of faith (Joshua 6:1-20). We may have circled our prayer-Jericho the full thirteen times, and yet the answer has not come. Why? Could it be that God is waiting to hear the shout of faith? Perhaps that is the reason the forbidding walls are still intact. He delights to see us step out in faith upon His naked promise."

Prayer time is a very personal time because God is personal. We are his son or daughter—that's the ultimate in an intimate relationship. "Ye have received the Spirit of adoption, whereby we cry, Abba, Father" (Rom. 8:15, KJV).

We should be aware that what we know about prayer individually does not always apply corporately.

I meet people who are so desperate for answers to prayer that they take their needs to a prayer fellowship: maybe a small group, maybe their church. And that is usually a good thing to do. That's biblical. All of us have had great times of prayer support when brothers and sisters in Christ have loved us and prayed for us, times when we have been able to bare our soul to them. There is nothing more helpful than to be supported, cared for, and loved in the difficult times of our lives. It is then that we know we are functioning in a supportive way.

But just as individuals can sometimes take their eyes off Christ and put them on circumstances, events, sensations, or the act of praying itself, so people can look to fellowship groups when they ought to be looking at Christ. The fellowship may be immature, or worse, all may be victims of the same teaching. Instead of finding deeper spiritual insights in a group, the person may find bad teaching, even allowing the group rather than Jesus to be his priest. There are dangers in not discerning when a group is misguided or when the group becomes a spiritual substitute for God. And it is evident from many experiences that a fellowship group may not be able to handle prayer needs because its own focus is off—it too is adrift and weightless. It is part of the problem. Thomas à Kempis explained why: "Some carry their devotion only in books, some in pictures, some in outward signs and symbols. Some have Me on their lips, but little of Me in their hearts." Not everyone, even in a group, has the heart relationship needed for prayer ministry. Some believe in prayer as a belief in prayer, not as a belief in the prayer-answering God. Others want to hear prayer needs, comfort and affirm, but they don't pray. "I'm thinking about you," they say. Still others are too insecure even to handle the prayer needs on a human caring or affirming level.

In a prayer fellowship, sometimes what could be a time for compassion and help turns instead into a time of destruction for the person or people involved.

I thought about this when I read an article by a pastor who insisted that people ought to share all their needs with others in the church so that the church could pray intelligently. Indeed, he said, the more severe the problem the more necessary to tell it to the church. He could be right—in theory—but in the real church, the human church, his advice could create chaos and great pain.

One evening a pastor met with his deacons about the serious misconduct of one of the church members. Most of the deacons sat quietly and listened; one wept. But one deacon let everyone know that he had "seen it coming," was not surprised by what happened, and was obviously eager for the meeting to end so that he could get out of the room and spread the news of the sin committed by his brother in Christ. The repair work on the damage he did took years.

What does a Christian who truly wants to pray with other believers do about discussing delicate situations in the church? We read articles which tell us that the church body has a right to know, that we are all members one of another, that the ear can't ignore the eye, that if there is a pain in the toe certainly it is felt elsewhere in the body. We know from Scripture that believers are one, that they must bear one another's burdens. We know that Christians are to care for each other, that there should be no secrets among us.

We know all of that about the body, but the body is rarely what it ought to be. Christians are still people in process; they are not all mature. The simplistic teaching that declares, "Tell all for the good of the church," ignores the hurt caused to the individual whose sins are broadcast because some in the congregation can't handle what they hear. Emotionally unstable church members can't be allowed to play fast and loose with the lives and emotions of other people. We are told by some that privacy violates the community, the essence of the church. But that is wrong. It doesn't violate the community any more than I violate a five-year-old member of the family by not telling him all that I tell a fifteen-year-old. The five-year-old isn't old enough to handle it.

One day our daughter, then a little girl, began to talk about an event in a parishioner's life which she should not have known about. "Where did you hear that?" her mother asked. And she told. It seems our pastor had shared private confidences of a parishioner at his dining room table. His children, hearing all of this, proceeded to tell their friends. The children didn't know any better; the pastor should have.

Parishioners, like children, do not all mature at the same pace. A pastor has to know who is able to handle information and who is not; he may even have to help the parishioner who is in pain and wants to share his burden to understand that. For example, wanting help I might be willing, even eager, to share my deep needs with the whole church. But not everyone can handle my needs, and the pastor or another mature believer may have to explain that fact to me lest I create a greater problem for myself by expecting some to take on more information than they can spiritually and emotionally handle. If we don't protect Christians from their own willingness to implicitly trust the body, they may end up hating the body, hating prayer, and hating God.

Maturity means that we understand the body and know what stress the body can take. We don't overload certain parts of it with problems it cannot handle. This calls for judgment, and no one is better equipped than a pastor or elder to know where the weaknesses are because they know the congregation. And if spiritual leaders have had psychological training, they also know any weakness in themselves. At least they should know, and if they don't it's up to others in the church to tell them. A pastor should know if he has a weakness for saying to his ministerial colleagues: "Well, I was praying with one of my members the other day, the president of the bank; he has a mistress. This is what I said to him. . . ."

He should recognize this weakness if he tends to illustrate his sermons with, "I was counseling someone in our church who has a problem with alcohol." Because if he does, a large portion of the congregation will mentally resolve, "I will never tell him anything." He should know that he must not only keep a confidence himself but recognize in the body others who can also keep a confidence so that there is a prayer support group in the church that people can trust.

The mature Christian is quite happy to pray for someone even if he doesn't know all the details. He knows that God understands the details. The mature parishioner will pray for the pastor and his counseling without knowing who the pastor is counseling or what it is about. The mature church member will know that when he is told something it is for prayer and not for gossip. And the immature, as they grow, will learn from the mature, until they too will be able to take on larger responsibilities of concern.

But as much as we work to develop the ideal congregation, we must know that we will always have some weaker parts. That's the nature of the church—it is a fellowship of less-than-whole people.

To assume that any are born into the kingdom full grown is to assume too much. It is to risk injury to members of the body. It opens the door to anger about prayer and the charges that "prayer doesn't work." Spiritual toddlers need help. That's not an insult, it's a fact. As they mature, they will walk, run, and not fall down as much. Then they too will be able to teach other young ones to walk. Until then, we can't expect them to be spiritual adults—particularly about real prayer.

When the focus is right, the reference is right, the obedience is right, and the relationship is right, we will no longer have to wonder, "Does prayer work?" or ask, "What if prayer doesn't work?" For we will no longer be looking at prayer, we will be looking at God —and his smile. And just as the astronauts work in space, each with reference to the same point, the church with Christ as the reference will be a place not of drifting souls but of firmly attached functioning people who can live and act.

In a weightless, drifting society we can pray because we know the One who answers prayer—and we know his directions are right.

F O U R
In the Joy of Ascending Moments

Ascending moments with God—what are they? The ever-rising approach to God in worship, in growth, in commitment. Is it difficult? Can I have such moments too?

Growth in worship is not like standing on an escalator or riding in a chair lift or being carried to a pinnacle by helicopter. Oh, no! It is movement that is sometimes as imperceptible as an inch-by-inch struggle to move with chained feet.

Friedrich Von Hugel spoke of the advice about spiritual growth given to him by an older man. He said it is like climbing a mountain. Each step is slowly taken with pauses to find the next handhold, the next level, the next rock on which to place a foot. There may be long periods between steps, longer times of encampment on rough ledges, sometimes whole days waiting for better conditions. Sometimes we wait in the clouds, sometimes in the dark, sometimes we huddle down in the rain or sleet or snow. No one scales great mountains unless he is willing to go slowly, waiting sometimes, thinking through each step, and then planting his feet firmly on what he knows is safe and solid ground. In the same way, those who think great spiritual heights are gained speedily do not understand Christian growth.

The *Twentieth Century Encyclopedia of Religious Knowledge* lists three forms of worship. There is the spectacular in worship when we think about those who are leading us, the subjective worship when we think about ourselves and what is happening to us, and the objective worship when we think about God.

The spectacular is soon finished. At best, we say of those who lead us: "My, weren't they good." It is much like going to a good concert or play. I remember being in a church where the choir anthem was a hymn of great adoration and praise. It contained the lines, "Not unto us be glory, O Lord, but unto thee...." I was led by the words to focus on God—his sovereignty, his right to be praised. The sense of his wonder overwhelmed me. But evidently others in the congregation did not hear those words because as the anthem was concluded, after the choir sang those emphatic words pointing to the Lord himself, the people applauded the singers; the choir director smiled and bowed.

Later, in another worship service, a man was reading a Scripture text that spoke of God, his power and his might. The person in charge looked over the shoulder of the man who was reading and saw that he was reading from the Greek text. No one else knew it, but he saw it and it was too much for him. His own insecurity or desire for praise apparently made him think that people would applaud the reader for his knowledge of Greek. So, though no one knew that the man was reading from the Greek text, as soon as he finished, the worship leader, without any reference to the fact that God's Word had been read, immediately turned the attention of the people from the Bible to himself. He stepped to the pulpit and said, "Oh, you're reading from the Greek," and then proceeded to repeat from memory a few Greek words that he had learned as a youth—words that had nothing to do with worship, nothing to do with the text read, but recited boastfully to show off. He was trying to impress us. He might just as well have said, "See what I can do!"

It was as if a bucket of cold water had been thrown on that warm experience of worship. God's Word was pushed aside for one man's own ego need. He hadn't really been listening to the Word in the first place, being occupied instead with the concern that people might praise the reader—and he wanted that praise for himself. A. Kuyper reminds us, "Just as the anthem of the Seraphim around the throne is one uninterrupted cry of 'Holy,—Holy,—Holy,' so also the religion of man upon this earth should consist in one echoing of God's glory, as our Creator and Inspirer. The starting-point of every motive in religion is God and not man. Man is the instrument and means, God alone is here the goal, the point of departure and the point of arrival, the fountain, from which the waters flow, and at the same time, the ocean into which they finally return."

Subjective worship, thinking about ourselves, puts us on the pedestal as gods. Eventually it leaves us with a feeling of failure because the more we think of ourselves the more we know that we are not God. But, reacting against subjective worship to have a true focus on God does not mean that we ignore ourselves or our sins. We can't take ourselves out of worship; that is impossible. On the contrary, we know our sins, and our failure is always with us. We know it because we compare ourselves to One who never fails. When we love God, our own shortcomings are obvious. And even our seeking to please God reminds us how much we, in fact, do not please God. But that involvement of self in worship of God is different from purely focusing on ourselves.

If we don't care what God thinks, only what we think or feel, it is because we don't love God. But even outright hatred of God, as bad as that is, is not so bad as ignoring God or putting ourselves ahead of God or trying to use God. To be lukewarm to God is worse than being cold or hot. "I know thy works, that thou art neither cold nor hot: I would thou wert cold or hot. So then because thou art lukewarm, and neither cold nor hot, I will spue thee out of my mouth" (Rev. 3:15, 16, KJV).

Lukewarm means we don't care. We have written God off; he doesn't matter even enough for us to consider him with any degree of emotion, be it love or hate. Subjective worship is as bad as spectacular worship; worse actually, for we have turned from gods outside ourselves to the god within ourselves.

In objective worship, looking to him and praising him, we discover true splendor—the spectacular of God. As we discover him we also discover ourselves, for we know best who we are to the degree that we recognize who he is. Isaiah knew that: "In the year that King Uzziah died I saw also the Lord sitting upon a throne, high and lifted up, and his train filled the temple. Above it stood the seraphims: each one had six wings; with twain he covered his face, and with twain he covered his feet, and with twain he did fly. And one cried unto another, and said, Holy, holy, holy, is the Lord of hosts: the whole earth is full of his glory" (Isa. 6:1-3, KJV).

J. Oswald Sanders noted in *Prayer Power Unlimited* " 'I have known men,' said Thomas Goodwin, 'who came to God for nothing else but just to come to Him, they so loved Him. They scorned to soil Him and themselves with any other errand than just purely to be alone with Him in His presence.' " And he further explained: "Dr. R. A. Torrey, who was God's instrument to bring revival to many parts of the world, testified that an utter transformation came into his experience when he learned not only to pray and return thanks, but to worship—asking nothing from God, seeking nothing from Him, occupied with Himself, and satisfied with Himself."

Himself! God only. The joy of ascending moments for us is as it was for Torrey and Sanders, and most of all as it was for our Lord Jesus who knew those moments with the Father.

But how do we come to the joy of ascending moments? How do we turn from spectacular worship and subjective worship to the objective worship of God? Should we seek the sensations of the emotions—an ecstatic experience? Satan can counterfeit those. God is more than that, even though sometimes we mistake experiences in ourselves as experiences with God. How then shall we worship in the ascending moments that place him before us and place us under the smile of God?

It takes desire, decision, and discipline.

First, we have to desire God. We have to want God in his way, on his terms, more than we want anything else. We have to desire the joy of the presence of God and then go beyond that desire, past the joy itself, to the presence of God. Is this mysticism? No, though mystics seek to capture it. Rather it is faith: a trust, a quieting down before God, a centering on him. It is the expression of our genuine desire for him, an expression made to him when we are alone with him wherever others can't make us less than sincere.

Second, we have to decide that we will seek God. Some people have the desire for God but they don't act on that desire. They wish for all that God is but do not decide to seek all that God is. We have to make up our minds and exercise our wills as surely as an athlete makes up his mind to train or a business tycoon decides he will be a financial success. The mind is given over to it as of first importance. The will is brought into positive action. Oh, that the mind of every person would focus on God by a willful decision to do so. What could God do with such persons?

Third, it takes discipline—working at it. It is something we desire. It is something we decide to do. We all discipline ourselves in some way. We do it all the time. I am currently seeking to bring my weight into line by shedding one pound a week. Emotionally I would like "instantly" to be fifteen pounds lighter, but it is going to take fifteen weeks. I've made up my mind to that, and day by day, with that weight loss in mind, I eat less and exercise more. The weight will not just disappear by wishful thinking. My mind is made up; the discipline is being applied.

In the same way I know that if I am going to meet certain writing commitments I must write so many hours each day. That is a discipline. I "will" write. The same is true for what is really important—the worship of God. The joy of ascending moments, like the climbing of a mountain, is an inch by inch process; it takes one day at a time. But the beauty of all this is that God meets us in our discipline. We find joy in these ascending moments even as we do what seems to be hard work in the self-discipline of seeking God. My daily morning time of worshiping God offers joy— now. But it wasn't as "joy full" before I disciplined myself to a daily meeting with God in the morning. I didn't do it then for good feelings it gave me (in the first weeks the only feelings I had were sleepy feelings), but for the anticipation of meeting God and wanting him desperately enough to discipline myself to seek him. It is what we all must desire, decide upon, and discipline ourselves to do.

In *Doors into Life,* Douglas Steere says: "Devotion requires continual nurturing, continual cultivation, continual renewal, continual beginning again, if it is to prepare us for the tasks this generation ahead requires. If this is true, then it is the task of the Christian religion not only to hold constantly before its members the necessity of their yielding themselves continually in acts of devotion to God, but also in encouraging them in the cultivation of these acts."

Why isn't it a part of our faith then to experience automatically the joy of ascending moments? It should just happen if we know God, shouldn't it? Why don't we just take to it, as a newborn colt when it is nudged by its mother stands up? Why isn't it automatic when God nudges us? It should just happen if we know God, shouldn't it?

This discipline of worship, of ascending the holy mountain of God, like tithing or honesty or faithfulness, has to be taught. And to be taught we need teachers who are themselves experiencing the joy of ascending moments with God. Unfortunately, many of our teachers are not.

It is difficult to teach worship. Even when we train men and women for the ministry of the church and the conduct of formal worship, there is little instruction in real worship. We teach homiletics and hermaneutics. We teach theology. We teach liturgy and the treatment of worship, but very little is done for those in training for the ministry of souls to help them experience first-hand something special for their own souls. What they don't know they can't teach.

The experience of having one's soul brought up close to heaven must be taught by showing it, doing it, and experiencing it. For only when they have experienced it can Christian leaders help others to do the same. I recall once saying to someone, "I haven't known worship in this church." He didn't know what I was talking about. The reason he didn't understand is that we were in the worship service together every Sunday. We went through a printed order of service, we sang hymns, we prayed prayers, we listened to a sermon, and we took an offering. But I hadn't worshiped God.

"Isn't that your responsibility?" he asked. Then he repeated the well-worn, "You only get out of it what you put into it." That's true, of course, but I also need to be led in worship. And in contrary fashion, I can be led away from worship. I need to be helped to see the Lord high and lifted up—the splendor filling the temple as Isaiah saw it. Those who thrive in worship, who are sensitive to the Holy Spirit, can help me do that.

When I realized that the man to whom I was speaking had no concept of what I was talking about, all I could say was, "If you ever worship, you will know what I mean." Then I quickly added, "That's offensive, I know. It sounds like a put-down but it isn't. It's like explaining the touch of a loved one's hand—you have to experience it."

My friend didn't understand what I was talking about; neither did the minister. He thought listening to his sermons was the same as worshiping God. He had no idea what worship was. I know he didn't because he would follow a great hymn of faith or a prayer of confession with an announcement about the church softball league.

But that's not really his fault. He never learned for himself the joy of ascending moments with God because he was never taught it. And he was never taught because he didn't have anyone to teach him.

In the training of Christian leaders, if we do not give them experiences in Christian worship how will they then lead others to worship God? At best, we urge ministerial students to attend chapel, and that is usually optional. As I recall my days in seminary, a number of students preferred to use chapel time to read the morning newspaper or play a game of ping pong. After all, they said, why go to hear another talk? They had no idea of worship; it was to them another talk, another lecture, a sermon, more preaching just like the classroom. They knew nothing of meeting God. And unless they have since learned, they probably can't lead their parishioners to meet God either.

I remember at my ordination service in Detroit a clergyman in that city spoke about worshiping God. He told the story of a minister showing his appointment calendar to the women in a Bible class. Every day and most hours of the day were filled with appointments. And all the people in that class were duly impressed. All, that is, except one little elderly lady who raised her hand and asked, "May I ask you a question? When do you do your thinking? When do you do your praying?"

We need to ask that of ministers who lead in worship and ask it of people who attend worship. When can God talk with you? When do you honor and praise him? When, if not in the congregation when there should be openness and responsiveness to him, can God speak?

In the average church service people visit with each other during the organ prelude. They aren't worshiping God. A few come late "after the preliminaries" to hear the important part, the minister's sermon. During a hymn which is meant to lead us to think about God, people look around to see who else is there. During the offertory prayer they fill out a check or search their wallets rather than present themselves to God, which is the first and most important act of an offering. Some think about their afternoon appointments, others muse about dinner or sleep off their breakfast. Last Sunday a man in front of me brought his morning cup of coffee into the pew with him and sipped it during the service. At least he stayed awake.

Norman Paullin, who for many years taught pastoral ministries at Eastern Baptist Theological Seminary, used to tell about a church organist who found a solution for morning talkers. Dr. Paullin explained to his class, "Every church has two people, one who can't hear and one who can't whisper, and they always sit next to each other. One Sunday morning during the prelude two women were busily engaged in conversation, oblivious to those around them whom they were disturbing. The organist, noticing them, gradually increased the volume of the hymn she was playing until the music was resounding through the sanctuary. The women, to compensate, increased their own volume until they were shouting into each other's ears. Then at the height of the crescendo the organist paused, changed the stops, and in the sudden silence the entire church body heard one woman shouting to the other, "I fry mine in butter."

Worship is not just being together; true fellowship, as the Anglo-Saxon word means it, is a "grazing together," a feeding in a common pasture. We are together, yes, but for a reason greater than just being together.

Worship is not just personal introspection, or we would worship our feelings. Worship is not even a warm glow, or we would worship that. We worship One outside ourselves. We concentrate on him, we praise him, we adore him, we hear his Word for he is announcing it to us. We listen in holy awe to the Word of God, for it is a part of that "all" of Scripture which is given by the out-breathing of God and is personally necessary for "my" correction and "my" instruction in righteousness.

How do we find the joy of ascending moments? We find it long before we go through the church doors; we find it upon our waking in the morning, we find it as we bow down before him in our own adoration and personal praise.

We are to be quiet before God. That is not an easy attitude, for most of the time we are so active that we are unable to relate to the still small voice. As activists, we are more interested in picking the fruit of the Spirit than in going to the root of the Christian faith. We mistake acting out the commands of the Lord in our lives (which, of course, we must do) with first knowing the One who commands. For if we do not first seek him, no amount of knowledge about him will substitute. For then what we are acting out are not his commands at all but our whims, our fancies, and sometimes Satan's subtle beguilings.

The joy of ascending moments comes not just because we are quiet, however, or we would seek only quiet and still not have God. In the quiet we would have wandering minds that could lead us into even greater trouble. Ours is to be a conscious focusing on God. When we do that, there come the ascending moments of the joy of God.

In *The Imitation of Christ,* Thomas à Kempis writes about rust-covered iron. Maybe we too are rust-covered iron, corrupted and encrusted with that which doesn't belong on iron. In that picture story is also a lesson to help us. He saw that rust will come away when the iron is put into the flames. To be clean, the iron had to be made red hot again. Those of us who are rusted, who are coated with the weakening agents of all sorts of encrustation, need to be put back into the flames of God again. Once more we need to be red-hot for God. When iron becomes clean, so much can be done with it; it is the same for each of us.

In worship we come to see not ourselves as the focal point, but God. It is not our talking at him that is important, it is our listening to him. It is what he says more than what we say that counts in the prayer that leads to worship. Our inner groanings are often more adequate for our approach to him than all of our polished speaking. His heart wants to beat with our heart. His desire is to draw us close enough to himself for us to sense that beating heart of God.

This is a quickening, these ascending moments of worship. God is interested in us. He wants to have our lives. He wants us to come into the inner place with him, to seek his direction, to find his purpose, to know his joy and experience his smile.

Should we not want that too? Should we not worship God rather than conduct worship services? Is he not worth more to the people he calls to worship than our attempted innovations in our worship services—some new angle, a new trick to please and draw crowds?

Let our affection be for him, the unchanging One. Adore him. Know that you need him for life, all of life. We do need God—right to the end of our days. In God's great heart is the longing to meet us, speak to us, and quietly raise us up to where he is, to those greater heights where we can see more of him and love him.

In that will come the great joy that he wants for us, the joy of meeting God himself in great ascending moments.

FIVE
Becoming Free

Augustine was a brilliant, faithful Christian born in the fourth century. To him the Christian church owes its safety, for he followed God's Word faithfully and taught the church during the onslaught of the heresies of Manichaeism, Donatism, and Pelagianism. He was a man of God, but he didn't start out that way. As a young man, Augustine lived for his lusts. At sixteen he was living with his mistress, having already enjoyed the lascivious pleasures of Carthage. At age thirty-one, then a teacher at the University of Milan, he was sitting thoughtfully one day in a Milan garden when he picked up the Scriptures and read, "Let us walk honestly, as in the day; not in rioting and drunkenness, not in chambering and wantonness, not in strife and envying. But put ye on the Lord Jesus Christ" (Rom. 13:13, KJV). He met Christ Jesus—and claimed him as Lord.

On Easter Sunday, at thirty-three years of age, Augustine was baptized into the Christian church. His experience with Christ was liberating. He had been confined in his sin; he was set free in Jesus Christ.

That is difficult for people to understand. They think the opposite. They see lasciviousness as liberating and the putting on of the Lord Jesus Christ as confining. Even some Christians, followers of Christ, still wonder if it is that way. This man Augustine, who studied rhetoric, mathematics, and philosophy throughout his life, said, "Believe in order that you may understand." When he wrote the twenty-two books entitled *The City of God,* he wrote of what he understood—the battle between two cities: the city founded by Satan and all of his wickedness, and the other city, the city of God. He wrote of slavery in Satan versus freedom in Christ. He knew the difference between the two.

In the book *Why I Am Not a Christian,* Bertrand Russell also talked about freedom. To him freedom means standing on our own two feet, looking squarely at the world, and making the best we can of life. He said that believing in God is not a worthy belief of a free man. Was Bertrand Russell free? Was he more liberated for having denied the existence of God than he would have been if he had admitted to it? Are we weaker for believing in the God of the universe and for willfully, purposely following him as our Master and King?

Or is it, rather, that it is the believer who knows true freedom because he knows the Source of life? Can one be free who is apart from God? How can any human being, subject to the forces of nature, living under the laws of creation, ignore the Creator, the Source and the Reason behind our existence? Some think they can; we know that to be in balance they can't.

It used to be that there were many "free thinkers" like Russell. There aren't so many anymore. The few who choose to be are mostly of Russell's vintage.

Having read a little bit, they have accepted his teachings. But there aren't very many. We have come too far and learned too much. We've discovered the holes in his thought.

I read Russell's book *Why I Am Not a Christian* twenty-five years ago. Recently I read it again. I found that though twenty-five years ago I disagreed with him on the basis of my own experience with God, I now disagree with him also through just plain thinking. Russell started with premises which eliminate, step by step, what he called the reasons for belief in God. But the reasons he criticized are the reasons of nonrational religionists. As a rationalist he had an answer for them. As a Christian I do too. But Russell did not have an answer for Christians because he saw Christians as people governed by fear. Having concluded this, he stated, as Lucretius taught, that fear is a source of misery to the human race.

But anyone who knows true Christianity knows that Jesus Christ takes away our fear. The Scripture is as true a description as it is a promise: "Ye have not received the spirit of bondage again to fear; but ye have received the Spirit of adoption, whereby we cry, Abba, Father" (Rom. 8:15, KJV). Russell took the fear of bondage and attributed it to Christians—then knocked Christians for that weakness.

Russell's conclusions are the only conclusions that he could have come to, because his premise was faulty to begin with.

Russell thought he was liberated. He wasn't. No person can be when his only source of thought, action, or belief is himself. He was confined by his own limitations—and those limitations included all the confinement of sin (the state as much as the acts).

Francis Schaeffer teaches that God *is,* whether or not we believe in him. God's existence does not depend on our belief in God. Ludwig Wittgenstein, the Austrian philosopher, taught that skepticism is senseless because it is built on doubt about a question. He states that if any question can be phrased at all then it can also be answered. But we cannot phrase a question about God. We cannot question the Infinite because our finite minds cannot grasp him. We can accept God, we can reject God, but we cannot question God. Only God can answer for God. He is beyond our proving. Therefore, skepticism about God becomes nonsense.

There are people who are skeptics, but they have no basis for it except that they want to be skeptical. That is their step of faith. The Christian chooses a faith step too. Abraham Kuyper said: "Verily Christ and He alone has disclosed to us the eternal love of God, which was, from the beginning, the moving principle of this world-order. Above all, Christ has strengthened in us the ability to walk in this world-order with a firm, unfaltering step." And in our faith steps we are secure. Why? Because in a firm way God enters into the life built on faith. Faith is an act of trust: trust yields security, and God in turn liberates the life committed in faith and trust. Liberty is by security made.

Soren Kierkegaard, the Danish philosopher, suggested in his writings that God can have nothing to do with an insecure man. That's a startling statement. He was referring to the child of God, the person who is in Christ Jesus. Kierkegaard was right. We are God's. That is not a wishful state; it is a secure state. What matters is not whether I am secure in "my faith" (for "my faith" is not secure), but am I secure in *God* by faith?

What does God think of me? Am I pleasing him? Am I faithful to him? Do I measure up to his standards? These are the important questions because they are already built on a conviction—the conviction that God is. That is the basis for courage, freedom, boldness in life. If we are insecure it is because we are not looking at God as the One to whom we belong; we are looking rather at ourselves or at other people.

Christians are "enslaved" to the One beyond themselves, the One not limited by their limitations. He is the One who came into this creation and made plain, "If the Son therefore shall make you free, ye shall be free indeed" (John 8:36, KJV).

How can we become strong, free, and courageous? What does it mean to be liberated? How are we to cope with and handle life? The answer comes from knowing a simple truth, that God is "for me." And on this basis we step out, we act, we venture, we live. The person who doesn't have that basis of freedom cannot reach the goal of liberation. He'll always be heading in the direction of further confinement.

I am free; Jesus set me free. That's a truism. Why should I reduce the full meaning of that by looking around at others and wondering about myself? Am I to be compared with other Christians? Am I supposed to be as successful as they are? As talented? As skilled? If God has made me, called me, and placed me where I am for his reason, if I am his child, adopted, loved, redeemed, chosen, blest, then why am I—why are you—so insecure?

There is only one reason for insecurity: we are not

looking at the Person who is our security, the Giver of it; we are looking at someone or something else. Sometimes we are even looking for evidence of God's security—and missing the security. That's why so many of us are not as free as we could be.

Fewer than twenty years ago, if we talked about obeying the Scriptures, participating in a Bible study, living by the Word of God, we were looked at askance by those who were not believers. Those who called themselves Bible-believing Christians tended to see a clear distinction between the world's view of God and the view of God as God explained it in Scripture.

Those called "liberals," who accepted society's views, were intolerant of any stand or view other than their own. It was a joke for years that the least liberal people were those who labeled themselves "liberals." Opposing them were fundamentalists who were known for a narrow view, particularly of Scripture, but unlike the "liberals," admitted to and even boasted of their narrow stand.

Today many fundamental Christians, once critical of those liberals who mixed together Christianity and a lot of secular, even pagan, culture, are doing the same with their own "fundamental" beliefs.

"How inconsistent, how immoral, how weak, how pagan!" fundamentalists used to say. "They have made their own religion. It certainly isn't Christian." But now many evangelical or fundamental Christians are doing exactly the same thing. There are Bible studies in almost every neighborhood, on college campuses (not only in every dormitory but often on every floor of every dormitory). There are Bible studies in factories, offices, and in government buildings. It's good that people are "into" the Word, but judging from their manner of life they are also into the world. The distinction between the Word of God and the teaching of society around them is no longer clear. In some cases, the Bible is being squeezed into the mold of the world.

Recently, I picked up a book on sex and marriage written by an attorney. In his introduction he stated that the book was written for New Testament Christians, and those who did not accept the teachings of Jesus Christ as authoritative would have difficulty understanding the spiritual concepts presented. I started reading the book. Inside, the author explained how the Bible is misunderstood when it talks about premarital sex being sin, how it is up to the individual to make that decision, how there are times when premarital sex is appropriate and correct. And all that he wrote he backed by Scripture—even giving some Greek texts and using references to well-known commentaries. His beliefs, he said, were based "on the Bible."

One day I had a conversation with two lesbian women who assured me that they were born-again evangelical Christians who believed that the Bible is the inspired Word of God. Yet when I turned to specific passages of Scripture about their relationship, they absolutely did not understand them. It isn't that they were purposely trying to avoid these verses, it was just that they saw no relationship between the Scriptures—what they believed—and their behavior which the Scripture condemns. At first I thought they were dodging the clear teachings of Scripture. But then I realized that they were not purposely disobedient, they were blind. No matter how I tried to show them the meaning of those passages, the application of the words escaped them. They couldn't see.

Later I said to some Christians, "Those two women weren't pretending, they honestly did not see. Are there also blind spots in my life? I too believe the Bible, but are there passages that I am not seeing because they relate specifically to me?"

I thought about that when I met a family that now only worships privately together; they want no fellowship with other Christians. They want to follow the Bible, they say, and in the churches there are too many inconsistent Christians. So the father leads their family worship every Sunday. They sing, they pray, they study the Bible together, sincerely wanting to follow Christ. But, I kept wondering, who corrects them? I asked, "How do you know when you are true to Scripture and when you are not?" The answer: "The Holy Spirit teaches us." They are correct in that the Holy Spirit who inspired the writing of the Word certainly inspires the reading of the Word, but he uses the body of believers too.

In the physical body the hands, the eyes, the nose, all work together. The body doesn't know its environment only by the signals in the feet or the nose. Isn't the spiritual body the same?

Several college students in a Bible study group asked me, "What can we do about one or two people in our group who want to dominate the Bible study and tell us what the Bible says because 'the Holy Spirit has revealed that truth' to them? How do we argue with them?" They had a problem, and it faces us all.

Even as we joyfully boast about the number of

evangelical Christians who are engaged in Bible study, we are recognizing also a rapid falling away from biblical morality, ethics, and truth. Teaching in the evangelical community is becoming a cacophony of sound. It's like an orchestra without a leader; each musician plays his own tune because the conductor is out of the room. There is no harmony, there is no orchestration, and, as a result, the musicians are unable to accomplish what they are supposed to do. They are not free to be musicians; they are unable to learn new arrangements. They can't do what they were meant to do.

People are searching the Scripture, but many are searching for what they want to find. The Bible warns, "This book of the law shall not depart out of your mouth, but you shall meditate on it day and night, that you may be careful to do according to all that is written in it; for then you shall make your way prosperous, and then you shall have good success" (Josh. 1:8, RSV). Meditate on the Word, yes! But why? "To do all that is written in it." That's our way to freedom. Our role is not to make our own way prosperous; that's God's role. Our job is not to work toward success; that's God's aim. Our task is to make sure that God's Word is in our hearts, that we meditate on his truth, that it becomes our food, our nourishment, our guidance. God takes care of the rest.

Jesus said, "You diligently study the Scriptures because you think that by them you possess eternal life. These are the Scriptures that testify about me, yet you refuse to come to me to have life" (John 5:39, 40, NIV).

We search the Scripture, then gather in with it all that is around us and call all the accumulation of it "inspired." We no longer present a clear, distinct message to our world. We are no longer biblical. The Bible says: "All scripture is given by inspiration of God, and is profitable for doctrine, for reproof, for correction, for instruction in righteousness" (2 Tim. 3:16, KJV). That means the Bible is to instruct me so I can be complete and perfect. That's what God wants, but that's not what Satan wants, and Satan seems to be getting his way.

C. Roy Angell, in his book, *Iron Shoes,* said: "Not only is there 'power in the blood' to cleanse us from sin, but there is power in the Son of God to break the bonds of Satan and set us free. Through the counsel room of every minister limps a continual stream of men and women who are handcuffed by some habit, some appetite, some sin that has made them prisoners, has hung chains too heavy to carry over their necks. They need to know that Christ, God's Son, can lift them up, make them straight, and break the bonds of Satan." And many of those "handcuffed" people claim salvation but haven't pursued obedience to its proper end—their freedom. We are to be servants; then we will be free. We are to follow him; then we will be bold to live. Only surrender will put us in the hands of Christ. He gives a certain message: "If the Son therefore shall make you free, ye shall be free indeed" (John 8:36, KJV).

An editorial in the now defunct *Watchman Examiner* stated, "Only if we accept the discipline of the free shall we be free indeed. He that persists in sin shall become the slave of sin. The luke-warm will worship the antichrist. The soft free are putty in the tyrant's power. They get that way by imagining he is not so bad after all."

I know a Christian who spends most of his waking time thinking about his investments ("How can I get the best return on my money?"), or what he buys ("I got a really good deal"), or on food ("The cooking in that restaurant is outstanding"). These are first in his thinking. He is a slave to those passions but doesn't know it. He justifies his thinking with words like "stewardship." He says, "I want to be a good steward with the money God gives me," and there is nothing wrong with that. Or, "I have to eat," and that is true too. But the emphasis controls him. It is his primary emphasis, his life, and each year it becomes more and more important to him.

A friend said to me: "You can tell what people worship by what they talk about." And he's right. I hear Christians talk about the value of their stocks. I hear Christians talk about their boats, their cottages —not just occasionally, as one does about anything in his life, but all of the time. Because it's what they are thinking about all of the time. We talk about what we are interested in. Nothing else is important. Scripture, and the obedience called for in Scripture, the obedience which truly liberates, is pushed aside. Even our responsibility to others in obedience to Christ is governed by convenience to ourselves or "what's in it for me."

Try something: explain to some Christians that maybe God didn't make a mistake when he put the natural resources such as minerals or good soil in the world. Maybe there is enough for everyone on earth but maybe God didn't intend that a few people in a few regions use it all while others go without. Try to explain that we ought to be using less. The reaction is sometimes outright anger. "I am not responsible for the rest of the world. I'm not even responsible for the poor in this country; that's what I pay taxes for." Or, "Who is going to take care of me if I don't look out for myself?" Or, "I'm a Christian; I have a right to all the things I want and need. I'm a child of the King; I ought to be able to live as the King's child." And when everything is all used up, well, they have an answer for that too. "Jesus is going to come and take us all home before there is ever any pain or suffering for us." They have it all worked out. Someone once parodied, "I'll build a sweet little nest, shut out the distressed, and let the rest of the world go by."

What does all this mean? Simply that we are not free. We are owned by all that we have made important. If God was important, then we would be obeying him and following him.

We are not able to cope and handle life knowing that God is for us because in reality we have made our own gods. We are enslaved by our wants, our lusts, our passion to satisfy ourselves.

As a magazine editor, I find increasingly that manuscripts coming in contain various roots of heresy. An author might be 98 percent faithful to Scripture, he may have a zeal and enthusiasm for God that is commendable. But there is error too, usually the kind of error that makes God what man wants God to be or adds something to go alongside faith or takes away from the deity of Jesus Christ.

These authors don't even realize what they have done because they are reflecting a Christian culture that doesn't recognize its assimilations from pagan culture. They have no teaching that gives them a balanced biblical theology, nor a Christology that is sound, nor a knowledge of church history that exposes problem teachings of the past. Nor is there even a willingness to note these problems. Never mind the heresies of church history, never mind that we flirt with them again, never mind that so many are claiming to belong to Christ who really belong to themselves, never mind that Christians are dissipating their lives and calling what they do "of God." These are captured people who want the assurance that "God is for me," without asking, "Am I for God?" The communion with God is gone; they are owned by other values and that entrapment has taken away their liberty to be free in Christ. A. Kuyper, in his book *Calvinism,* said: "Only he who personally stands before God on his own account, and enjoys an uninterrupted communion with God, can properly display the glorious wings of liberty."

Where are those who are yielded to the Scripture on the basis of what the Scripture says, not what people want it to say? Where are the Christians who will subject themselves to the whole counsel of God? Where are those who will read church history and theology to see what other people have wrestled with in the past? Where are the theologians of the day who can help us learn that we can't baptize culture and call it Christian? Where are the books that teach us something more than the faith of pleasure, that do more than tell us what we are entitled to, that we ought to have a happy life, a pleasant sex experience, the best stocks—all in the name of Jesus?

Where is our freedom? We have managed this far, many of us, because life has been fairly comfortable. But what will happen when the crunch comes? When persecution comes to us and we find that we are not snatched away? When we, like many Ugandan Christians, are martyrs too? Where will we be when the dissipation of the present age catches up with us? Already we are beginning to see the signs of failure in those who have been living without disciplinary controls. And how will we function if we choose enslavement on an even grander scale?

Only when we can be trusted to read the Word on our knees will we be free. Then God will be with us on *his* terms. He will be able to trust us with his power; he will be our God; we will be his people.

When Peter came out of prison, the angel said, "Go, stand and speak in the temple to the people all the words of this life" (Acts 5:20, KJV). He was to speak all of it, not part of it. He was released from prison for a reason. We are released from prison too. We are released from our own fancies about God and from the prisons of our own wants and desires. We are free and we have the liberty of declaring by our lives, our actions, as well as our words the whole counsel of God—not only in the church but in the marketplace as well.

Secular life was all around Peter, but he told the people about the Christ-life, the eternal life, the whole message of God. So we are called to declare that message in the marketplace, in the temple, wherever we are. That's why we were let out of the prison of Satan's bindings. We are to stand as declarers of the whole counsel of God in word and deed, proving by our lives the gospel of true freedom.

We're released from prison to do what we're told to do. Whether it results in our success or our death, faithfulness is the key to freedom. Faithfulness is the way to live every day, under the smile of God.

SIX
When People Don't Like You

Satan doesn't bother very much with those who stay away from God. He does bother those who want to come close to God because he knows that what the Bible promises is true: "Draw near to God and He will draw near to you" (James 4:8, NASB). And he doesn't want God to do that. Often the "higher" we go spiritually—that is, the closer we draw to God—the more we will have to bear what is unpleasant. Satan will put pressure on us.

This doesn't mean that we are to bring pain upon ourselves; Christians aren't masochists. It doesn't mean we live apart from people, as if living for God means to be self-righteous.

This does mean that to be like Christ is often an offense. Jesus Christ is an offense to people, and by living in Christ we may be an offense too, although we are not to be *offensive*. There is a difference. If people don't like me, it had better be because they don't like Jesus, and they see Jesus in me.

Jesus had admirers. There were some who liked what he did. But in the crunch, those in authority would not accept him. He was acceptable to most if he didn't go against anybody. But when he did (and to be faithful to the Father he had to), the pressure from those who were Satan's followers came down on him.

If you are faithful to Christ, you may be pressured by Satan too. To obey Christ is to take up a cross and follow him. That cross is an ugly object, a thing of execution. If you take it up, don't be surprised if people want to crucify you on it.

But a Christian who is faithful, who is hated for Christ's sake, though he is knocked down can still pick himself up again. He doesn't stay down because he knows that other people's opinions of him don't really matter. For the Christian, God's opinion counts.

Remember: "For the Lord God is a sun and shield: the Lord will give grace and glory: no good thing will he withhold from them that walk uprightly" (Ps. 84:11, KJV). And if troubles come, don't worry about it; you know what is happening—God owns you; keep going. Hear what Scripture says about you: "The steps of a good man are ordered by the Lord: and he delighteth in his way" (Ps. 37:23, KJV). Those words are for you.

So are these: "I will lead the blind by ways they have not known, along unfamiliar paths I will guide them; I will turn the darkness into light before them, and make the rough places smooth. These are the things I will do; I will not forsake them" (Isa. 42:16, NIV).

And God also promises, "When you pass through the waters, I will be with you; and when you pass through the rivers, they will not sweep over you. When you walk through the fire you will not be burned; the flames will not set you ablaze" (Isa. 43:2, NIV).

Christians are going to be disliked because they love

God, and for another reason too. They are going to be disliked because they care about other people. Watch what happens when Christians try to do something about the destruction of people by alcohol. Watch what happens when Christians try to prevent the pornography that often leads to the abuse of children. Watch what happens when Christians speak out for the poor or against racism or for reduction in armaments or against the consumerism that is the religion of so many.

There is an assumption that Christians don't know the world. I remember several years ago discussing abortion with a Christian counselor who was trying to stop it. She said, "You know, they think we are out of our depth because we are older, not married, don't have children, and can't understand the situation of an unwanted pregnancy. But when these women have an abortion, feel the trauma of having committed murder, think about suicide, and seek to assuage their mental pain, they don't go to the abortionists for help, they come to us. I wish the abortionists would get some of the 'after' counseling that we get. But they don't, and these women are taught that an abortion has no more lasting impact than having the dentist pull a rotten tooth. Those who encourage abortion don't see what we see. They don't have to counsel the suffering; they believe their own propaganda because they don't see the results. We do, and we fight, and then we are told we don't know the problem. In fact, they are the ones who don't know."

It's always painful to listen to the sneers of unbelievers who want to put down Christians. "You hide behind God," they say. "You don't know reality." "I understand life; you wouldn't understand life. You'd be shocked by some of the things that I know about," they boast. "You wouldn't go to the places I go; it would overwhelm you if you knew what life was really all about." They speak as if all Christians are people who sit under church steeples with blinders on.

Yet I watch Christians. It is the Christians, because of the love of Christ, who work and keep on working with these same sneering people when they are too drunk to stand up. It is the Christian who, enduring their abuse and their vomit, tries to help them keep from killing themselves by driving them home and putting them to bed. And he does it knowing full well that when the person is near sober again, he is going to say to the Christian: "You can't cope with reality; you have to have your God." And the Christian takes the abuse and watches that person go back to his bottle, all the time yearning for him to come to Christ for new birth.

It is the Christian who works with the heroin addict who tells him that he doesn't really know about life when all the time the heroin addict, with his low threshold for pain, is killing himself because he can't face himself or his life.

It is the Christian who works with prisoners in penitentiaries, caring for inmates who to most of society are forgotten people.

Even as he binds up wounds or cooks a meal, perhaps for the person who is criticizing his beliefs, the Christian knows that what he is doing is not for himself (he already has the assurance of heaven, gained for him not by his works but by the cleansing blood of Christ), but for the weak person he is helping—and he remains silent. Thomas à Kempis said: "Do not concern thyself overmuch about who is for thee or against thee; but take care to act so that God will be with thee in everything that thou doest. Keep clean thy conscience, and God will defend thee, for he that receiveth the protection of God, no man's malice shall be able to harm."

But don't be a phony about it. John Dunne, in 1610, wrote about the "pseudomartyr," the person who wanted to be considered a martyr without really committing himself to anything that would earn it. People like that are more interested in their reputations than in the obedience that gives that reputation.

When people don't like me, it's my responsibility to be sure that I'm not somehow trying to be disliked. Having watched a particular woman antagonize people, I mentioned to her what she was doing. She angrily denied the very thing that I saw her doing. In fact, she then went on the attack, saying she was not the problem, but all the people around her. She couldn't see how people were standing back from her, afraid to speak to her lest they upset her, or saying, "Don't be upset, I'm only trying to help you." She was always the martyr, but a martyr only by her definition, not other people's.

There are times when people don't like us because we are, frankly, not likeable. We need to look at ourselves honestly, ask others about our ways, and make adjustments in our behavior.

I've noticed how other perceptive people can guide me in ways I've not thought about. People who know and care for me can tell me how I act and what I communicate better than I can determine for myself. We need the advice of other growing believers if we are going to continue to be healthy, maturing, stretching believers ourselves. No matter what your circumstances or how you are hurt as a Christian, as long as you have examined yourself, counseled with others, and prayed, you can know this: God is with you.

Tucked away in 1 Chronicles 4 is the description of an interesting man named Jabez. His name sounds like the Hebrew "pain" or "hurt." His mother gave him that name because she cried, "It hurt me to bear him." Think what a burden she put on that child! His name was a description—he was a hurt to her. Children must have mocked him on the street and called him "Hurt." Adults would think of pain when they spoke of him. He could have been destroyed by that name.

But Jabez, by his example, gives us all hope. Scripture says: "And Jabez called on the God of Israel, saying, Oh that thou wouldst bless me indeed, and enlarge my coast, and that thine hand might be with me, and that thou wouldest keep me from evil, that it may not grieve me!" (1 Chr. 4:10, KJV). He cried out to God and God undid everything that his mother and other people had done to him. The Scripture says: "And God granted him that which he requested."

People may be unkind; God is not. There is cruelty in the world but not in the heart of God. Others may despise; God loves. Others may put down; God builds up. And even this one named "Hurt" God saw as honorable.

That little story of Jabez appears in the midst of all the genealogies in 1 Chronicles. It is a passage so many skip over in their reading. Perhaps God tucked it in there because he wanted us to find it and take courage. Jabez did what all of us can do—seek God about the matter.

Trust God to work out for you the messes that others put you in. Believe God as Joseph did, certainly as Daniel had to. They believed. They trusted, and trust is the opposite of worry. Worry will consume you. Worry cripples. Worry about your situation is a denial that God can handle it. No one, no matter what burdens he or she places on you, should be allowed the chance to cause you to stop trusting God.

Lisa was crying when she told me, "Nobody likes me. I don't belong anywhere: I don't belong at home, I don't belong at school, I don't belong in the youth group at church. Nobody likes me."

Lisa was fifteen, and as she tried to express her feelings her body shook with deep, deep sobbing. As we talked, several things became evident: she could see that her feelings about not being accepted by other students in school and by other young people in the church were really based on her not feeling accepted in the first and basic unit of her world—her home.

"Why don't my parents like me? Why won't they accept me?" she cried.

She told how they were always scolding her: "You don't appreciate all that we are doing for you." And when she went to her parents wanting to talk about her thoughts, her worries, some of her bewilderment about life, they pushed her away with, "Oh, we've all been through that," or "You'll get over it." And if she questioned, "Why won't you talk to me?" they would reply, "We talk to you," and then go on with what they really wanted to do or talk about.

The reason Lisa was talking to me about this was that she had dropped hints that people in her church had picked up—hints that she could see no reason to keep on living.

Lisa is a victim. And although I didn't say so in exactly the same words, she is the victim of her parents' inability to hear her. They can't understand why she doesn't appreciate all the things they purchase for her. They can't see that she could possibly have a problem. To them she has all the material things a young girl could want. But Lisa made some discoveries as we talked—not discoveries that I gave her but discoveries she found within herself.

Her parents had grown up in poverty. Both had longed for the things that money can buy. Both had gone without. In their own way they were giving her what they never had, showering on her all of the things that they had wanted. They couldn't understand why she wasn't happy because those things would have made them happy when they were young.

Her parents had forgotten the things they *did* have as children. They didn't have much in the way of material goods, but they did have a family life. Parents and children talked to each other, listened to each other, cared about each other. Today, as adults, in their busyness, they don't give Lisa what she needs more than anything else—a family: parents who love her, encourage her, and give her counsel when she isn't sure which way to go.

The people who mean the most to her, her mom and dad, aren't helping her to see that she is a pretty neat kid. They are pushing her away. From their actions she is picking up signals that are just the opposite to the signals her parents think they are giving— signals of not being liked, of not being accepted.

Lisa is going to have a hard time, but she is learning that her parents probably aren't going to change. They are still going to measure her happiness by their concept of happiness and be bewildered by her nighttime crying. Now, with help, Lisa is talking to other people. She is finding an older woman in the church who can be her "mother" or a mature couple who can be parents to her. These are people with whom she can talk freely, friends who will tell her whether or not she is making good choices. They will put some fences around her ethical, moral, and spiritual choices. They will give her love.

And maybe, and it's a big maybe, when she no longer has so great a need from her parents because she is getting love elsewhere, maybe with fewer demands placed upon her, she will be able to give to her parents some of the affection that *they* need. And maybe they will return some of it to her in the way she needs. And maybe the vicious cycle will be broken.

There are a lot of Lisas in our world, people who are saying, "Nobody likes me." The signals they are getting reinforce what they believe is true.

There was one other word of comfort I could give Lisa. "God likes you; God loves you." On the authority of God's own words about his love, I could tell her something of the deep dimensions of God creating her and knowing her and understanding her and loving what he created. I could show her that God likes what he put into her and likes what he is going to do with her life.

As we talked about the future, we talked about the day to come when she, more than many, will be able to say to another young person, "I know. I understand what you are saying because I have been there." And Lisa is beginning to see that her feelings are not feelings that can be read about in books or taught in classrooms; they have to be experienced to really know. But because they have been experienced, she is going to be a Christian counselor who will teach about the loving nature of God. Someday she'll help many others who are going through what she is going through now.

We may not be liked, truly not liked. That realization can destroy us, or we can build on it and become secure people of God.

In Scripture we read that the Apostle Paul, a saint of God, had real problems with young John Mark. Mark didn't make it as a missionary, and there were flare-ups over it—hard feelings. Perhaps Mark felt sorry for himself or wondered if there would ever be any value to his life. Having been given a chance to do something with one of the greats in the church and having messed up, and having created such tension that there were splits in the missionary society over him, he knew, "Paul doesn't like me." And Paul didn't, at least not then. But whatever it was that God did with John Mark, he changed and grew. He wasn't thrown on the refuse heap. God didn't give up on him. We know he didn't because later Paul said, "Take Mark, and bring him with thee: for he is profitable to me for the ministry" (2 Tim. 4:11, KJV).

We need to know that not being liked is not an end; it may even be a beginning. It depends on what we do with it and what we believe about God's redeeming and rescuing help.

Do we lie awake at night worried? Worried because of what somebody said about you or what is going to happen tomorrow? "What might happen if. . ?" you wonder. Then you get out of bed and get a glass of milk and sit in a chair wide-eyed, or you pace the floor. All around you is quiet; the family is asleep, the night is still. You sense that you are caught in a maze trying to articulate for yourself all of the ramifications of the confusing things that can't be articulated because they are too mixed up.

Wide awake? Do you know what? So is God. He is there. He wasn't asleep even before you got up. He neither slumbers nor sleeps, the Scripture says. And he is watching. "The eyes of the Lord are upon the righteous, and his ears are open unto their cry" (Ps. 34:15, KJV).

Paul said of Jesus Christ, "He carries out and fulfills all of God's promises, no matter how many of them there are; and we have told everyone how faithful he is, giving glory to his name" (2 Cor. 1:20, TLB). That can be a description of what Jesus does for each one of us.

Do people dislike you? Who are they? What if they did like you? Would there be a different problem, a much bigger one? Would you have compromised to win their favor?

No one who carries the name "Christian" should be obnoxious. No one should be lazy, or destructive, or a bringer of pain. But having forsaken all to follow Christ and being aligned with his Word, taught through the prayerful counsel of other believers, go out and live under the smile of God. No matter what people outside Christ say to you or about you, remember what God told Isaiah: "Fear thou not; for I am with thee: be not dismayed; for I am thy God: I will strengthen thee; yea, I will help thee; yea, I will uphold thee with the right hand of my righteousness" (Isa. 41:10, KJV).

Did he mean that, or didn't he? Isaiah knew that God meant it, and he believed him. You can too.

SEVEN
When I Am Pressured to Do What Is Wrong

The life of a Christian is like the flight of a spaceship. His new birth is the ignition of the rocket. He begins slowly, but it's a start. And as he gains momentum, moving higher and higher, some of the once-important support systems drop away. The craft needs to be free to move. The rocket thrusters, the hooked-up launch equipment, is needed on the ground for lift off but not needed when the craft truly flies. For the Christian in his new life that is true also. There is much of the pre-launch life that he doesn't need anymore. He is out and away and moving. He is set free to fly just as he was designed to do.

For the non-Christian that is not so. He too is designed to fly, but he chooses to stay on the ground. He likes the hookups, the support systems, the security of lots of fuel, the constant maintenance of his needs. He sees the small world of activity around him as the real world, and the people running here and there to add this or adjust that as the reason for his existence. This is his universe. It is his world and he understands it. There are people ready to analyze his problem, people to fuel his large capacity to consume, experts to repair some physical breakdown—everything he needs—focusing on him. He is the center of all activity. But he doesn't fly; he doesn't even get off the ground. He doesn't go anywhere.

Yet from his base he may be quick to sneer at the little spacecraft that is launched and flying. It is small and it appears to be alone. The heavy, consuming craft on the ground calls to the spacecraft above, "Real life is here. Real life is what is happening around me." He can't and won't believe the spaceship which says: "I started there too; I know where you are. This is better —this is what we were designed for!"

The Christian soars in the orbit of God. The unbeliever calls from his launch pad and insists that his base living is real living. And for him it is, because all he has ever known is his base activity. He has never flown. For him, this is the real world and he assumes that because we are not part of his base-locked mentality, we do not understand where he is. We are "out in space somewhere," out of touch with the real aspects of life. He cannot grasp the fact that we were once there on the ground too, and have been launched into something better. Now we are flying in a new dimension but he can't believe it. How could he? He can't conceive of another dimension, especially one without all of the familiar activity around him. And he can't conceive of our freedom from the weight of all that once held us down too. He doesn't understand because his "big" world isn't big at all. It isn't that he sees more; it's that he sees less. He is unable to see the bigger world beyond his own immediate sphere. He is, as someone once put it, "as a maggot in a piece of cheese, who, because he lives there and it is his food, thinks that that is all there is to the universe because it is his universe."

Those who stay on the ground aren't happy about those of us who fly. They look at their own design and wonder, "Is there more? Should I be flying too?" But being the center of their world, where the servicing is so good, they don't really want to fly. Still there is that invitation, that reminder every time we fly by, that those soaring free of earth's gravity do have something, a larger panorama than those on the ground can see. So they stay where they are.

And still convincing himself that he is where the best is, he tries to drag the flying ones down to him. Occasionally he succeeds and "proves" that he is right —for a spacecraft fallen from space, lying on the ground, is a helpless thing. It has neither flight nor ground support. The base-living person only needs one such example to prove his theory about himself and his life. But can he bring one down? Can he convince these flying-free ones that it is so much better where he is? Since he doesn't want to fly himself, can he find some flying ones to join him on the ground? If he can, he will not be so uncomfortable. There will be one less to relay descriptions of the awesome view that is reserved for fliers.

Christians are made to fly with God. If you're flying, don't be caught by those who pressure you to come down and become one with them. Nehemiah asked: "Why should the work cease, whilst I leave it, and come down to you?" (Neh. 6:3, KJV). The Christian can also ask: "Why should I stay on the launchpad? Why shouldn't I soar into space? Why shouldn't I be free? That's what I was made for! Why should I be entangled with all of the things that hold the unlaunched rocket in place?"

Christians will always be pressured by those who don't want believers telling them that there is another way to live. Those on the ground don't want to know that there is a better "view" and that they are missing it. They want to stay below and focus on themselves. But they would be a lot more comfortable about it if believers would join them.

Whether it be a little or a lot, don't compromise with those on the ground, the unlaunched ones, even for a minute. At your office, refuse to take company supplies for your personal use even though you will become a threat to those who do.

In your neighborhood, refuse the parties that always end with various couples in various beds, even though you will know it the next day when your neighbor won't speak to you.

In your life, refuse the pressure to measure your value by what you can buy.

There has been in every era of history pressure to compromise, to engage in sin, to worship man instead of God as the center of everything. This has always been and always will be because of man's gullible buying into the lie of the snake. "For God doth know that in the day ye eat thereof, then your eyes shall be opened, and ye shall be as gods, knowing good and evil" (Gen. 3:5, KJV). Man won't admit it, self-protection will not let him admit it; there is even risk in admitting it, for either he turns in trust to God or knows that he is destroying himself. Dietrich Bonhoeffer, who suffered under the Nazis and then died at their hands, said of those who put men at the center of the universe: "The man who is faced by God's commandment as demand is thrown back upon himself and must live in this way. Man now lives only out of his own self, out of his knowledge of good and evil, and in this he is dead."

This pressure from Satan has reared its head in every generation, and the tendency for Christian reaction is the same in each generation too. And so also is the need to classify or label all the sins and evil around us. It is so easy to do because it doesn't require much thought just to label and react.

Classifications are simple; we like slogans because they're easy to work with. Every politician knows that. Every advertiser knows that. We like to lump everything together in order to get a handle on it. But when we use labels, we ignore the fine distinctions between various points of view.

In evangelical circles our current label for all that is evil is "secular humanism." Man's sufficiency unto himself *does* turn him from all that is moral, decent, and kind. Man in his fallenness isn't just separate; the correct word for that which is the opposite to "holy" is "profane." Profanity is the lifestyle of trying to live apart from God. Man apart from God becomes the personification of a swear word. Profane man becomes the opposite to the good of God. In saying no to God, he puts himself up as his own god; that's profane humanism—to be assessed, avoided, fought against, and judged.

But we should not attack to the point of hurting the humanist as a person. Many humanists believe what they believe because they are searching. If they try to pull down the Christian it is because they are miserable in their search. We must realize that, perverted as he may be, man is still the beautiful creation of God, the reflection of the divine nature of the true and living God.

Honest humanism, because it begins with man (for that's the only place man can start in his quest, even in a quest for something larger than himself), is searching humanism. Therefore honest humanism doesn't have to end with man; we can help the humanist look. Help him in his searching. Help him with his own beliefs that he needs to question, because if he does, his conclusions will lead beyond himself. God is truth, God is holy, God is beautiful. Any steps in seeking those attributes of God bring man toward God; they open man to God. For if we help him touch truth, beauty, and love, he will see for himself that there must be a larger source of beauty, truth, and love than he has ever known before, one certainly larger than himself.

We must provide an opportunity for the humanist to find the well from which the living waters are drawn. Even humanistic scholarship will bring people to God if it is indeed *honest* scholarship—a seeking after truth and wisdom—because God alone is absolute truth and absolute wisdom.

It is becoming more and more obvious that it is the true thinkers, the honest men and women, who are turning in believing faith to God. It is the little minds, the people who haven't gone far enough, the ones with but a little learning, who have yet to sense the reality of God. That's why we hurt them if we throw labels at them. They don't have to search any further when we react like that. Their little bits of truth satisfy. We actually isolate them and interrupt them from the pursuit of real truth. We hurt rather than help if we do not allow them to pursue their thinking to logical conclusions.

Why do we react? After all, they cannot hurt God or dethrone him. God does not need a defense. We need instead to get close to them, help them go on, encourage them, lead their thinking. Honest humanism may be their first step. If they explore the streams of life, perhaps they will come to the source of life; certainly they will more likely do that if we take them further in their thinking. We need to have more to do, not less, with the narrowness of secular humanism. We need to work constantly to enlarge their view. We need to know where they are, why they are there, and lovingly help them take the next steps.

But that doesn't mean compromise or even tolerance of the actions of the unredeemed person. It means caring for and helping him, not turning him off or insulting him. It doesn't mean wallowing in man-centered worship with him, gorging on human lust with him, or worshiping his gods with him. We are first and foremost bound to God himself; there is to be no compromise with that. But if we are secure in God, the temptations won't hurt us. It isn't temptation that is our downfall anyway, it's the giving in to temptation. Don't insist that the world stop tempting with its secular humanism. Instead, go deeper and deeper into the biblical truth of God and obey him. This will bring far more to light because the Holy Spirit is in us working. We mustn't forget where we are or what we have. We are salt and light. It will be known.

Show the better way, the higher truth. Don't insist that people must stop practicing "secular humanism";

they have nothing else to practice. Rather, show them God's truth, the attractive life in Christ. If secular humanism is having its day, it may be because many who claim the name "Christian" have in fact become "Christian humanists." They don't want secular humanism to reign unchecked, but they don't want the absolute rule of Christ in their lives either.

Soren Kierkegaard, the nineteenth-century Danish philosopher, wrote about the Christian's purity of heart. The pure heart is a heart that is bound to God. God is pure and the heart tied to that purity is pure. We are tied to him, connected with him, one with him; we are—consider the vine and the branches —attached to him. The question is never how pure should I try to be, rather the question is how closely attached to Absolute Purity—God—do I want to be? James 4:8 encourages us to draw near to God. That's our work, drawing near to him, and thus to draw near to his purity. If we are near, the purity will be there in us. But ours cannot be a drawing near to God in words only, it must be a drawing near in deed and in fact. It comes in our daily lives through the practice of the presence of God. It comes from the transformed mind. The desire for God is as the hart panting after the water brooks (Ps. 42:1). A thirsty soul and a pure heart are what God wants. Stay close to God, seek his presence in all of this life, be closer to him than to anything or anyone else.

H. C. G. Moule said, "The Christian's aim is bound, absolutely bound, to be nothing less than this: 'Let the words of my lips, and the meditation of my heart, be always acceptable in thy sight, O Lord, my

Rock and my Redeemer' (Ps. 19:14). We are absolutely bound to put quite aside all secret purposes of moral compromise; all tolerance of besetting sin, for the sad reason that it is besetting. With open face we behold the glory of the Lord, and ask to be changed (2 Cor. 3:18) at any cost, all round the circle of life, into the same image. We cannot possibly rest short of a daily, hourly, continuous walk with God, in Christ, by the grace of the Holy Ghost."

When I am urged to do the unclean thing, the impure thing, when immorality or illegal behavior or selfish grasping is put before me, I can't blame those who tempt me with all that. They don't know any better. Still, I don't have to be a part of it.

I can work for better television, seek the end of pornography, commit myself to the care of the poor, the elderly, the disenfranchised, the dispossessed. But I can't criticize those who cause these problems; they probably don't know any better.

Because I have another perspective, because I know what life can be, because I know what we were designed to be, I need to live an example of that life to the fullest, not only for its life-giving renewal hour by hour for my sake but for the example it gives to encourage a struggler who needs to find this life too. For those reasons I will not, I cannot, compromise.

Dietrich Bonhoeffer said, "So the Christian lives from the times of God, and not from his own idea of life. He does not say that he lives in constant temptation and constant testing, but prays that God may not let the time of temptation come over him."

Scripture is clear to those of us who are determined

that we will be governed by it. First Thessalonians 4:7 states: "For God hath not called us unto uncleanness, but unto holiness" (KJV).

God does not want us to live in impurity; he did not create us for that. He created us for holiness, for his sanctification. It isn't that he calls us to develop our own sanctification; that is not something we can achieve. He does it in us. The sanctifying One is the Lord Jesus Christ. We are already in him, and he works out in us that sanctification. Therefore, because we belong to the sanctifying One and he is sanctifying us, we don't engage in impurity. We can't do it, not because it does anything to God, for God is not touched by us, but rather for what it does to us. God knows what impurity does to us and it breaks his heart. He loves us too much for it not to break his heart.

People are confused, of course, by teachings such as these, for they think of impurity as something from which to abstain on their own strength, and of sanctification as something to achieve. We are being sanctified; if we are in Christ, that's what he is doing in us. We are clean, whole, complete, justified, and since that is so we do not practice impurity. We are in Christ and he is pure; therefore, it is contrary to what we are in Christ to be impure. We cannot practice what we are not. That does not mean that we will not fall into impurity, trip into it, or wander into it when we take our eyes off the True Light—it happens regularly. We are not freed from the flesh yet, we aren't in heaven yet; we will stray. But we will not *live* in impurity. That is not our calling. Our calling is to live out what we are as justified and sanctified ones in Christ Jesus.

Jesus said, "If any man will come after me, let him deny himself, and take up his cross daily, and follow me" (Luke 9:23, KJV). Self-denial is more than self-control. It is the ability, purposely and decidedly, to say no to self. It is a willingness to turn our backs on something and to turn our faces toward something. It is not just controlling or regulating by laws what is corrupting, destroying, or hurting us; it is a purposeful turning away from these. We do it for God's sake and for our own sake.

That's the way we face down what tempts and corrupts. And at the same time we lead others out from it, showing them a better way, encouraging them to look at what is better, and not letting them go. We hold on and help but we don't get dragged down with them. A man who joins another in a ditch can't pull him out.

Don't be trapped into believing that all is right in this world. There are those who will try to teach you that and even sometimes use Scripture to do it.

It was Gottfried Leibnitz, writing in the seventeenth century, who spoke of a world that was good, a world of truth and joy, a world that has in it the essence of perfection. What then of sin and pain and struggle and suffering, you ask? Well, he tried to explain that by saying it is similar to the grain of wheat falling to the ground and dying so that it can produce more. It is what Jesus spoke about. In fact, Leibnitz taught that such pain contributes to man's good. For as man suffers and feels pain, fruit comes. It leads him on to an even greater perfection.

Leibnitz's observation is true enough in one sense, for many people are often stronger because of suffering. But that is only an explanation for what happens to man, not for what man is. In fact, the world is not more perfect for all of its pain. Nor is man. Man is not getting better nor will he, for he is part of fallen creation. He is not living as Adam did before the fall. He is not in communion with God. And even when redeemed and given life and wholeness in the centrality of Jesus Christ, the decay and the corruption that attacks him from every side is still there, surrounding every individual. People will use drugs, alcohol, sex, the deadening effect of a television set, or even the busyness of everyday life as devices to distract them from reality. This world is painful. For some the threshold of pain is higher than for others, but the pain is still there. And man does not get better for it. Liebnitz was wrong.

God offers himself in the midst of an anti-God, painfully fallen environment. It is peace amid turmoil, rest in confusion. In the despair, he is the reason for being. And man senses it. If he were content in his own private separation from God, why would he not rest in his separateness? Why does he work so hard to bring others down to him? Because others who are not like him are a threat, a reminder of another way, another world, another life. And he knows it.

Our standing firm as believers in the true God is a beacon light; it is salt. To compromise, to become one with the world—whether it's in our cheating, our divorcing, our aborting human lives, our lying, our conniving—is to say to the world, "Your suspicions are wrong. There is no better life than what you have. We are only pretending about what we have; we are faking it. Your inner longings for God are all misunderstood." We tell man that there is nothing better than what he has, and in doing so we leave him without hope. For even though he attacks, tempts, urges us to compromise, he is always wondering deep down inside if perhaps we are right and he is wrong. He must be shown light, for only when he sees a light can he hope to have that light too.

There is a better life, a better view, one free of the compromising controls of the corruption around us. We can enjoy, indeed revel in, the "more" of God, and say to those missing it: "It's here; launch out, be free, come to the living God and live—fly!" The hope that we offer, the better life we seek for others, is the life which amid the tragic offerings of the confused and the lost is lived under God's smile.

God is your defense, he is your armor; he is your righteousness too, in all the temptations that come. Hear again the words of Bonhoeffer: "From heaven the Lord gives to the defenseless the heavenly armour before which, though men's eyes do not see it, Satan flees. *He* clothes us with the armour of God, *he* gives into our hand the shield of faith, *he* sets upon our brow the helmet of salvation, *he* gives us the sword of the spirit in the right hand. It is the garment of Christ, the robe of his victory, that he puts upon his struggling community."

And again, he who faced the world and died said: "He who loses courage because of the suddenness and the awfulness of temptation, has forgotten the main point, namely that he will quite certainly withstand the temptation because God will not let it go beyond that which he is able to endure. There are temptations by which we are particularly frightened because we are so often wrecked upon them. When they are suddenly there again, we so often give ourselves up for lost from the beginning. But we must look at these temptations in the greatest peace and composure for they can be conquered, and they are conquered, so certain is it that God is faithful. Temptation must find us in humility and in certainty of victory."

Know this: you wouldn't have to face any temptation if you had already given in. If you were already the devil's possession, he wouldn't have to work so hard on you. But you are "someone"—and if the snake invaded the garden of purity once, he will do it again and again. He has so much to lose if he doesn't. Remember the One who said, "Be of good cheer; I have overcome the world" (John 16:33, KJV). That's his word for you.

Good cheer! That's for the soaring one. Enjoy the view of your Christian life. It's what you were designed for. Don't ever compromise it or give it up. You are set free to fly. Now do it.

EIGHT
As God Goes to Work with Me

"If you think most young people have goals, you don't know what is going on."

The man who said that to me one afternoon employs dozens of young people, many of them entry-level, first-job people, some in their middle or late twenties.

He was telling me that my picture of young people who want an education, a career, etc., is the exception. "Most," he said, "only have short-term goals focusing on the next payday and immediate thoughts of how they will spend their money. A long-term goal is a new car or a trip. Such things as a house, an education, training for a trade, are not part of their thinking."

Then he added, "And I'm talking about Christians. Just because a person accepts Christ as his Savior doesn't mean he has purpose in his life."

That conversation came about because I had expressed two emotions—my pleasure over a few people who are willing to work and give their best, and my exasperation over a larger number who want to be paid an attractive wage but have neither the commitment nor the discipline to work for it.

My "education" about people, their willingness to

work, to sacrifice, to discipline themselves for long-range goals was broadened by that afternoon's conversation. But that education had begun some months before. I was discovering that Christians can be lazy. In fact, when I gently corrected a slothful worker, I was met with the challenge: "What difference does it make? Jesus is going to return soon." My only response was, "When he does return, I'd like to be found working."

Once when we were looking for new staff at *Decision* magazine I found myself asking: "Where are all the people who are willing to work?" A friend commented: "With the job situation the way it is, I should think a lot of people would want to work." My exasperated reply was, "No, people do not want to work. They want a paycheck but they do not want to work." Eventually we found just the right people—hard-working, committed, faithful Christians who sense the calling of God in their work—but it took awhile to find them. There are a lot of people, including Christians, who are only thinking about what they can take from a work situation not what they can put into it.

Ask any employer if that is true. Most companies have to program additional help into their labor force just to make up for those who tend to be "sick" on Mondays or who take extended coffee breaks, read a newspaper in the stockroom or leave early on Fridays, all to the cost of thousands of lost hours a year. Statistics published by the personnel departments of large corporations show that these "lost" hours raise production costs by as much as 15 percent compared to five years ago. And Christians are just as eager as non-

Christians to find a way out of doing the work they promised to do when they were hired.

Christians, even though they refer to their vocation as God's calling, will still complain about their jobs, complain about the atmosphere at work, complain about their salaries, become easily fatigued—all while telling others (often on company time) that they have a living, vital relationship with Jesus Christ.

Scripture says that when David was appointed by Saul (1 Samuel 18:5) he "went out and was successful wherever Saul sent him" (RSV). David did what he was told to do. He wasn't seeking acclaim or the praise of men; he did his job. It doesn't take long in any organization to discover who is willing to work, who has a servant attitude, who is committed to the task before him, and who is not.

There is no difference in attitude toward one's commitment to a calling, a job, a company, an organization, and a commitment to God. For work is a way of expressing our honesty (earning a day's pay for a day's work instead of expecting to be paid for work not done) and faithfulness (going the second mile, doing the extra task instead of doing just enough to be noticed).

Unfortunately—and it is part of a need to "appear" to be faithful—there are Christians who try to fool their bosses. They are the ones who cannot work behind the scenes; they must always be near the people in authority to make sure that they and their work are noticed. They work hard when they are being watched, but disappear when the boss is on vacation or out of town on a trip. If another employee needs help, they find excuses not to give it because there will be no personal gain or recognition for them. "Why should I help him?" they say. "That's his job."

As David did his job, he wasn't paying attention to who noticed. But he did it so well that people did notice and started praising him. As a result, Saul turned on him. That can happen. Our job is to be faithful and hard-working even though fellow employees may turn on us. They may not like it when someone does a better job or gets a higher salary for work well done. They want "equal" pay, but cannot or will not discern that, everything else being equal, they are not worth what the hard worker is earning for the simple reason that they do only enough to get by. It is a delicate thing to work hard in order to be faithful to one's calling while knowing all along that other employees who want the same pay and the same praise resent the hard work that earns it because it shows them up. Living for God as a worker is not easy. David found that out.

We say, "Yes, but there came a day when David was successful and had the recognition and power." That's true, but that was years later. And it is worth noting that it was after he had success and power that he tripped up and sinned so seriously. We desire the bigger job, but if we get it we also run the risk of falling into the larger temptations.

Maybe God does us a service in keeping us where we are. The faithful Christian is one who works hard and trusts God to do the promoting if there is going to be any promoting, because he also trusts God to give the power and ability to handle the accompanying temptations and pressures.

Notice something in Scripture about a little-known

worker, a hardly noticed man of God. When it was necessary to replace Judas Iscariot, bringing the number of apostles to twelve again, two men were put forward (Acts 1:23). One was named Joseph called Barsabas, also named Justus. The other was Matthias. When the disciples prayed over those two men, they acknowledged that God knows the hearts of men and that God is the one to choose and ordain who should have an office and who should not. They acknowledged that God makes an apostle. The lot fell to Matthias. He was chosen.

But what then became of the "second" choice? And what can we learn from the "winner"? Who were these two men? Who was Joseph called Barsabas? Did he also follow Jesus with the twelve? What had made him so outstanding that he could be put forward as one of two choices in the first place? And how did he feel when the lot was cast and he lost? When it was stated, "By God's decision, you are not the one," did he sulk? Did he say: "Why is Matthias so special?" Did he remind the other disciples, "We do the same work; I follow the Master too—why him? Why not me?"

Or was he mature enough to recognize that God chooses some for one work and some for another? We assume that he was mature enough to understand that, or he would not have been mature enough to be put forward as one of the two in the first place. He would have seen that the office of apostle was not something to covet, that the ministry of being one of the twelve was not to be sought for purposes of power or prestige or personal gain. He would not, had he been named one of the twelve, been praised in the assemblies of the rich or the powerful. He would not have had special privileges, or been sought after as a banquet speaker, or been asked for his autograph. When he was put forward for the ministry of an apostle, it was a position that would mean suffering and perhaps even a brutal death. Could he have handled that? Ten or twenty years later would he have had whatever was required to remain a faithful teaching apostle? We will never know, for God made the choice. God chose Matthias.

And who was Matthias, this one who was chosen? We don't know because neither Matthias, the one chosen, nor Joseph, the one rejected, was ever mentioned in Scripture again. So even the one who gained the office did not get the acclaim of a Peter or a Matthew, or a James or a John. Was he jealous? And if so, what would he envy? Would he envy Peter's imprisonment? John's exile and death?

Matthias was chosen; Joseph was not. Neither was heard from again. We know nothing of their families, their education, their ministries, their ages—just two names.

God chooses us. Some are chosen to have one ministry, some to have another. Some, like Peter, are chosen to be noticed more than others. Some, like Matthias, not to be noticed at all.

We each have a holy calling. In Christ we follow God's choice. We have put ourselves forward to be available for God's choosing. We did that when we committed our lives to Christ. As Christians, we are chosen for ministry. No matter what that ministry is —whether it's physical labor, office management or medical missions—God calls; we obey. He directs; we faithfully work. And we do so for as long as God commands, following him even more than we follow our careers. For all of us know that once decided how he will use us, God can still bring change to our lives at any moment. Surely Joseph, the one called Barsabas or Justus, was doing something different vocationally before his name was put forward as an apostle. He had years of experience doing something: obeying God, feeding his family. Maybe he went back to his trade. For a brief moment perhaps he wondered if he was going to have a "mid-career change," only to settle back again into the calling that he had before. God wasn't steering him in a new direction after all. But he was willing. God could have chosen him.

Matthias did make that mid-career change. Was he a carpenter? A fisherman? Did he have a business? Whatever he was doing, he left it for the ministry of apostleship. He was ready to be chosen and God did choose him. Each of us, in fulfilling our daily vocation, needs to be ready for God to make a choice. James makes it clear in his epistle that none of us can say, "Tomorrow we can do thus and so"; we do not know what tomorrow brings. Tomorrow is God's and we are God's. Vocationally we must be faithful and ready.

That's why it is a sin to be lazy, refusing to do what we are hired to do. Matthias, whatever he did before, could not have suddenly become a faithful apostle if he was not first a faithful worker in his regular field of work. God wouldn't have chosen a man who was always looking for ways to get out of work. Peter was a skilled fisherman. He was not highly educated but he was not unlettered either. He had the full course of synagogue school training, which meant he had language study, history, Bible memorization (for Jewish boys the entire first five books of the Bible were committed to memory), grammar, geography, and mathematics. He knew at least three languages—Hebrew, Aramaic, Greek—and perhaps Latin also. He knew the principles of management as well as the skills of operating a family fishing company—including the bookkeeping, pricing, purchasing, equipment handling and repair, weather, currents, and the habits of various species of fish. All these were part of a highly skilled craft. All these equipped him to be an apostle by God's grace, the senior minister of the first church in Jerusalem, then an overseas missionary, and finally a pastor in Rome.

Peter was ready. You can be too, for whatever work God calls you to do. God knows you. He knows your likes, your dislikes, your skills, your abilities. He knows because you're no accident. God knew what he was doing when he made you, he knew what he was doing when he gave you the gifts and talents that he has given you in a unique combination unlike anyone else. He knew what he was doing when he called you into your vocation. And, if you're a committed Christian, you can say with confidence that he knew what he was doing when he brought you to himself through Jesus Christ. He paid a price for you, a price that is above every price. You have great worth. Is there then any moment or any circumstance when he will not care for you and help you and lead you?

God knows what he is doing in your life now. God has placed you where you are because he wanted to place you there. He has given you the work that you have because he wanted to. You may think that you just stumbled into what you are doing, but there are no surprises with God. Surely when you started doing what you are doing now, God's mouth didn't drop open in amazement. Surely he didn't exclaim, "I didn't know he was going to do that."

In the overall plan of God, he is directing you and directing those who work with you whether he gives your job to you for a year or for your whole career.

I know a Christian teacher who spent sixteen years in a small town in Michigan's Upper Peninsula, living on low wages, struggling with inadequate equipment, but working there because God led him there. And how he influenced those students' lives—not only at school but on Sundays in a little Sunday school held in his home. He worked there suffering through those cold Michigan winters because God wanted him there, influencing not thousands, but classes of just a few. One of those classes graduated seventeen young people. I know how that teacher influenced the valedictorian of that class; I know how her life was changed. I know how she has gone on to serve Christ. I know, because she is my wife.

We are to pray, obey, and serve. We are to be ready as were the early followers of Jesus to leave all and follow him, to be ready to have a career as a carpenter or as a tax gatherer, to be ready to follow in a new role because that's what God wants.

This is true for those who stay at home too. There is no less discipline to homemaking, mothering children, doing traditional "at home" ministry than there is working for a paycheck outside the home. In fact, the disciplines are tougher because there are few immediate rewards. One works as a homemaker out of absolute commitment to a higher calling than a paycheck or company fringe benefits. One works because "God has placed me here."

When the Apostle Paul began his work for Christ, he was ready to obey. And God took over from there. God used him to change the world. We have our Christian roots in that faithful man. His missionary work produced a body of believers who are our spiritual forefathers.

Paul had a career before he met Christ. But after he met Christ his career was changed. God could do what he did with that man's life because Paul was ready to obey. It wasn't an easy life that Paul led; it certainly wasn't without pain. Whom do you know who has suffered as much as Paul did? Whom do you know who has been beaten as many times, imprisoned as often, been shipwrecked, hungry, so physically ill— whom do you know who is like that?

Yet, to have a vocation as Paul had, with the hand of God upon him, walking under the smile of God, we envy him. We see him as an example to follow. The question for each of us is never, "Am I qualified, capable, or willing to be an apostle like Paul?" The question, rather, is "Am I, as Paul was, ready? Am I faithful right now?"

My vocation, my ministry, is to work under God and also to work alongside those whom God has appointed in ways that he has not appointed me. God has the right to use some people one way, others another way. That's his prerogative. God will use whom God will use. We can fight against it, complain about it, scream, kick, call him unfair; or we can relax and fit into the pattern of God.

In 2 Kings 6:1-7 that is what happened. Elisha was

God's anointed, and God gave him tremendous powers. One day a man lost his axe head in the water. It was a borrowed axe head. He called on Elisha to help him. He didn't assume that he had the power himself, but he knew that God had anointed Elisha with special power. It was God's choice to use Elisha. Elisha, in the power of God, raised the axe head. But notice something. Elisha didn't go in and pull the axe head out of the water after he made it float. The man had to do that himself. Elisha made it float; that was his gift. But the man had to retrieve it. He had to do something too.

That is so in our lives. It is wise to recognize who has a special anointing of God. But we do not envy them, nor covet their gift; we recognize the gift, go to them to use their gift. But we do not expect them to do everything, or to do what we can do ourselves. We respect what God does through them—their abilities, powers, even the miracles that God works through their lives. We ask them for help, trusting that God is giving that help through that person. He is only a piece of clay, a tool, but God is using him.

God has given you a special gift and others will ask for your help. It is not your gift; God gave it to you and God expects it to be used. And with our separate gifts we work together. That's what the body of believers is all about. This is what that man did with Elisha, and this is what we do when we work in conjunction with those whom God has anointed in a different way than he has anointed us.

Don't take credit for your gift. Don't assume that the power seen in your life is in yourself. God has his ways that are beyond our understanding. We act, using what he gives for his sake and the sake of others, and every day God goes to work with us. Work with him, work for him, be faithful in your vocation, and you will please God. That may not mean a larger paycheck or more company benefits—for there is no correlation. But it will mean that each night you will be able to go to sleep knowing that you did your best for God, and that if you died in your sleep and never returned to your job you would have left a work well done. And by the time your co-workers know you are gone you will already be standing with your Lord and will have heard the greatest of all commendations, "Well done, thou good and faithful servant . . . enter thou into the joy of thy Lord" (Matthew 25:21, KJV).

NINE
With Family Love Around You

By the time our son was four years old, he was asking
to go fishing. "Go fishing with me, Dad," Grant
would say. But except for a few times, I wouldn't take
him.

We lived in Highland Park, New Jersey, where I
pastored a church, and although a park bordering the
Raritan River was close to the house and had places
along the shore where we could drop a line, I knew
that there were only a few scavenger fish in the river.
To me there was no point in fishing. It certainly wasn't
worth my time. I was busy; I had a congregation to
look after.

"Go fishing with me, Dad," Grant would say. And
my response was almost always the same: "Not
today."

So the weeks went by. Grant didn't beg, he just
asked. And most of the time I had too much to do, or
so I said. Being four years old and trusting, he believed
me. He didn't know, nor did I, that God was getting
ready to teach me a lesson.

Wanting to be a good minister, wanting to help
people, I enrolled in the Master of Theology degree
program at Princeton Seminary, majoring in counseling. One day a week I took classes learning how to
be a better counselor. Now, having added the Princeton studies to my work load, I was really busy.

"Go fishing with me, Dad."

"Not today, Son. Daddy's too busy."

One of the requirements for the degree was a year of clinical work at a psychiatric hospital. I went to the hospital each Friday and spent the whole day. As students we talked to the patients, analyzed each other's counseling techniques, and spent intensive times in sensitivity training under the direction of a chaplain-supervisor. I didn't need the latter, I thought; I was already a good pastor, just trying to be a better one. Certainly I was sensitive to people. What could that chaplain–supervisor tell me? Besides, he had admitted that he was divorced and didn't believe in the divinity of Jesus. How could he teach anything to a happily married, committed evangelical Christian?

But the chaplain didn't ask me about my theology or my biblical beliefs, he asked about my relationship with my son. And after a few minutes of listening, he laid me bare.

Roughly, our exchange went something like this:

"Don't you even hear your own son?"

"Of course I hear him. He wants to catch fish. But that's a waste of time. There are no fish in that river worth catching."

"Did it ever occur to you that catching fish isn't really the important thing to him? Your son wants to go fishing with you. He wants to be with you. He is asking for your companionship. He wants to be with his dad."

That chaplain—and Grant—had me. And, as I was quickly learning, so did God. My orthodox theology couldn't substitute for my availability to my son. I was cheating Grant of the one thing in life nobody else could give him—me. God had given Grant to me; he was entrusted to me; the gift of father-son togetherness had to come through me.

The only difference between Grant and that chaplain was that the chaplain could state bluntly to me what my trusting four-year-old couldn't express. But I began to realize that Grant could feel, and what he had to be feeling was rejection. I was saying, "Daddy doesn't have time to go fishing." He was hearing, "Daddy doesn't have time to go fishing with you." Grant couldn't put that into words, but the chaplain could and did.

Fortunately, God understands a father's change of heart. He can correct a bad start. He can overrule inept parenting. And he did.

I tried to change my ways with my son. We went fishing together and did some other things. But, I wondered, was I starting too late? Guilt rode me hard. *I've failed,* I thought. *He'll be scarred.*

I didn't have to punish myself, but I didn't know that then. One day, years later, I timidly asked, "Do you remember, as a little boy, how you always wanted to go fishing with me and I said I was too busy?" I steeled myself for the response. Here was his chance; he had probably saved all of his pent-up anger —now it was going to come out.

Grant grinned. "I guess I'd forgotten about whatever times we didn't go fishing. I just remember one time when we did go and you snagged your line on the opposite bank. I thought that was really funny."

And together we laughed at me.

We can all tell stories like that. We know our own weaknesses, we know how we wish we had done some things differently. We want to live with our families under the smile of God. And God in his goodness wants to help us. He knows if we want faithfully to serve our families and if we do not.

No one who has his eyes open needs to be reminded of what is happening to the family. When it goes, so will society. The family is society's basic unit of love, security, learning, and cooperation—a unit blessed by God.

In your circles, who helps Christians when family problems are first getting started? Do people keep silent or simply talk behind each other's backs? Who addresses the temptations and weakness that we all have, and speaks openly and candidly without condemning but without compromising either? Who is saying to believers, "Your family is your ministry too," and saying it before a wayward drift begins?

The sacred vows of marriage and the responsibility of building a Christian home are too often treated in a secondary manner by church members and church leaders. How many of us in our family lives are examples of what Christ wants the home to be? How many of us as parents are able to say with the Apostle Paul, "Be ye followers of me, even as I also am of Christ" (1 Cor. 11:1, KJV)? Each of us might ask ourselves, "What would be the example set for our world if I could say that too?"

As it is, not only are we not teaching each other (if that were the only problem we would simply be struggling along with no teaching), but we are being taught by everyone else—and we follow their examples very well.

We need clear direction and reinforcement from

each other and from the Word of God if we are going to be distinctive examples of what God intends families to be. We need help to stay married, and encouragement to build Christian families. God expects it and we will answer for our casual, even cavalier treatment of God's order if we ignore him. His teaching and our responsibility to each other are meant to be high priorities.

Why have a Christian home? Why, in the light of all the divorces and remarriages among us, do we even stress God's order? Why faithfulness; why the struggle? Why not do what some other people do—just split and run? No one seems to be less respected for it. Why fight for what may be only our concept of traditionalism in home and marriage?

The answer is this: we have made a vow to God. Each of us has stood before God and said words similar to "in sickness and in health, for richer or poorer, for better or worse, till death us do part." Each of us made that promise to another person in a pledge before God.

Yet when the electricity seems to be gone or someone else seems more attractive, some are willing to break that vow. That cannot be done! God speaks clearly about promises (Deut. 23:21, Eccl. 5:2-6).

I have to be aware that if God cannot trust me to keep a vow no matter what the difficulties, he may never be able to trust me in anything else. In the instructions to husbands to live with their wives in understanding and honor, Peter warns "that your prayers be not hindered" (1 Peter 3:7, KJV). If there is any explanation for the weakness in some churches, can it be, at least in part, due to the hindered prayers of those whom God knows will quickly break a vow made to him?

This sounds harsh and in one sense it is. But note, it is true that we can make mistakes and God will heal. It is true that the love of God is greater than any of our failures. It is true that if we fall we don't have to stay down. It is true that if we break God's Law, he doesn't push us aside and say, "That's all for you!" God doesn't treat people like that, nor should we. But he doesn't smile at flagrant sin either, especially when he knows that we are more interested in our own pleasure and personal satisfaction than in obedience. Only by being trusted and trustworthy can we build a lasting Christian marriage and family relationship. Because only then can all the strength of God be on our side.

There is strength in total commitment; it is the strength that comes from the success of overcoming. But the undisciplined, the weak, the escapist will never find it—he will never overcome; he will never know what God has for him in the true intimacy of marriage.

One evening, after both our son and daughter had had an early supper in order to be on time for their own planned evening, my wife and I had a quiet dinner together. We didn't go out; we stayed in the kitchen. She didn't cook anything difficult or fancy; it was just a casserole that the children aren't fond of but we are. We ate by candlelight, leisurely talking about everything and anything that was important to us. Then, when dinner was over, we had devotions together, holding hands. It was an intimate evening— just ours—and we both sensed the presence of God and a deep, deep love. That comes from commitment and years of trust.

It takes years to build that kind of relationship, which is the reason that many couples declare that what they have after twenty-five or thirty years of marriage is so much more special than even the excitement of their newly married life. Ephesians 5:28, 29 frankly admits that there is self-love in that, and that is quite appropriate: "So ought men to love their wives as their own bodies. He that loveth his wife loveth himself. For no man ever yet hated his own flesh" (KJV).

If we believe that, then it explains why some in the body of believers seem to have trouble getting along with their spouses. They dislike themselves. They are the ones who are looking around for someone else, someone who will give them value, some reason for being, some stature in their own eyes. They need someone who will appeal to them because they are so insecure in themselves that they do not know who they are, they do not know their own self-worth. They do not love themselves, and as a result cannot receive love from the one with whom they live. But the one who knows himself and his needs, and wants to love, can be loved and give love. There are many spouses longing to give love to the mate who is looking elsewhere. And as long as one is looking for another to give him the security and value that he craves, he will never really open himself either to his mate or to God. If it is true on any level, it is true on the level of marriage: "He that loveth not... [one] whom he has seen, how can he love God whom he hath not seen?" (1 John 4:20, KJV).

Think of the impact on the world if married couples who are Christians would give visible testimony to the love in their marriage because God is love and they love God. Many people don't see God and do not know that it is possible to have God because they don't see God in overflowing love, especially in marriage.

A strong Christian marriage has an impact which will be felt in generations to come. We offer a heritage to our children in our faithfulness to our spouse; there is a legacy in love that we give them. Their home, the framework in which they try their wings, needs a commitment that is not shifting. They need a solid footing. They have to have models and security in the home to achieve emotional strength and spiritual depth. When they have it, their own security makes them healthy and able to give the same to the next generation. But it's difficult to relay to others what they never get themselves. There is evidence of that in third- and fourth-generation divorces, battered children, and socially destructive adults.

It is in the home that children learn to pray. It is in the home that they learn what love is, how to give it and how to receive it. It is through the exchange of love between a father and a mother that children themselves understand how to be a father or a mother. They learn marriage by seeing it in the workshop of the home. And experiencing human love, they have a basis for accepting God's love. If their world is shattered by separating parents, where will they turn? We know all of the excuses made by those who leave their children and their spouses. And we know the heartache in many marriages where couples stay together for appearance's sake or for the children. That's why love, care, and nurture is needed—not condemnation. But duty is connected to joy. When a husband and wife fulfill a duty each to the other, they also fulfill a duty to their children and joy does come.

"But," you say, "Christians too have roving eyes." It is "acceptable." And therein is one of Satan's most delicious traps. Passing fancies are shallow. What can some other person offer? Suppose I pursued someone else because I thought God wanted me to have "more." Suppose I found another woman who to me was special. Suppose I married her. She would never be able to trust me! For as long as I lived, no matter what I promised her, she would always know deep down inside that I have not only already broken a similar promise to another woman, I have broken a promise made to God. My word would be worthless. If I went after her while I was still married, how would she ever be secure in my promise that I would not do the same to her? She could never be secure. She could never relax and be truly herself. She would never be at ease, or comfortable, or secure, or at peace. She would always be uncertain, always wonder, and would never have the true openness that makes a marriage strong.

Who knows me better than the one who has cried with me, prayed with me, and knows my soul? Who can give and take with me better than the one who has shared life with me? The "passing fancies" can never do that. If a person is concerned to obey 1 Corinthians 7:33 about how to please his spouse, that spouse will be the center of all his thoughts and desires. No outsider will ever be able to enter into a fenced enclosure that two have built together.

It is not just simple reasoning that makes us obey the teaching that God wants us to stay married. It is the matter of not willfully being disobedient, of slapping God in the face and saying, "No, I won't." Jesus said in Matthew 19:5, "For this cause shall a man leave father and mother, and shall cleave to his wife" (KJV). A married couple is one flesh, and one flesh cannot be divided. If we try to cut it asunder, or encourage others to cut it asunder, what will we say to God? Will we say, "You didn't mean what you said"? Will we tell him, "I thought you were joking"? Will we try to face him down and say, "I thought you were telling a lie"? Will we become theologically verbose and declare, "You don't understand me; I still trust you to save me for eternity but I just can't trust you to save my marriage"? "I will be faithfully yours forever in heaven but not during these years on earth"?

We have a responsibility before God for our families. The Apostle Paul stated, "Believe on the Lord Jesus Christ, and thou shalt be saved, and thy house" (Acts 16:31, KJV). Before God, my faith involves my family. I am responsible.

The statement, "As for me and my house, we will serve the Lord" (Josh. 24:15, KJV), is one that a Christian needs to make. When a Christian refuses to make it, when he determines that his salvation is strictly personal and the salvation of his children is strictly personal too, he is opening the door to a fragmented Christian family that carries over into the church and into society. It promotes breakdown of the family; it opens the door to divorce. As a husband and father, if I am responsible only for me, and "my soul is saved," then I can convince myself that I am free to leave my wive and children because I have no responsibility

spiritually for her or for the children. I have deter-
mined that each of them stands individually before
God and I am not obliged to be involved; they are
God's business, not mine.

But God has given me my family. He has placed
them in my care. Their souls, it is true, are his apart
from me, but I am a teacher, the one to pray for them,
the one to whom they look for counsel, an example of
Christian living. Can I be satisfied with my personal
salvation in Christ if there is not also for generations to
come a dynasty of Christians following after? Christians must face this.

How can we live this Christian life of obedience? By
singleness of eye, by one desire—by obeying.

Life is so vast; it has so many facets and sides that,
like a multifaceted diamond reflecting in so many
different directions, we can neither grasp it, understand it, nor live in it all at the same time. Our lives are
too complex. Temptations and pressures come from
many places. We can only focus on one place and call
it the focal point of our lives, the center. That center
is the place of my praying, the place of living out my
Christian life, the place of my security. That place is
home.

In my work, I travel a great deal. I am geographi-
cally in many places but there is one focal point in the
world, one place that is always my reference point—it
is home. No matter where I am, no matter which con-
tinent it is, how many miles from home, my traveling
is possible only because emotionally I am back home.
Nairobi is not so many miles from London or New
York; it is so many miles from home. Sydney is a

certain distance, a certain time in travel from home. Tokyo is a certain number of hours and plane stops from home.

One night, after being away from home for three weeks, a colleague asked, "What time is your flight in the morning?"

I replied, "The first flight out, 7:40."

"What time do you have to get up to be at the airport on time?"

"I'll be up at five."

"Why don't you take a later flight? Why get up so early?"

"Because I'm going home."

Home is where my heart is. And I think God teaches a lesson through that. He teaches a lesson about the heart's longing for heaven. That is where God is. Someday I'll really be Home. Only a few more years of travel on this earth and then I'll be Home. I'll be secure within the warmth of Home. And in the vastness of life, like the vastness of the globe, there is that focal point—Home. Every distance, every moment of time, is referenced by the word "Home."

God knew that. He gives homes now and he gives a final Home. He puts the temporal and the eternal together in our hearts. Don't shatter your home. It is there that you will experience the smile of God. And it is there that you will learn to live out the training in all the dimensions of yourself that you will take with you when you don't have to journey anymore and are truly "Home."

Live with family love around you now. Don't destroy it. Home is your training ground for eternity.

TEN
Growing When You Are All Alone

It was raining in Osaka, Japan, that October morning, and my mood was as gray as the sky. Work kept me busy most of the hours, and some days I was in my hotel room only to sleep. But this rainy morning I felt alone. I was trying to write and I couldn't. I was feeling sorry for myself. I was homesick.

Then, as I sat looking out the window, I began to think of the other people alone in that city of millions. So many were like me, only they were lonely all the time. There are plenty of interesting things to see and do in that city: there are the shops, the restaurants, the parks, the canals, for this city is called "the Venice of Japan." And yet people who are lonely like me really have no interest in doing anything; we let the hours go by, just sitting—feeling depressed, dull.

My head ached, too, maybe from the weather, maybe from anger at my situation or myself or God. I reached for the New Testament that was on the table in front of me and started thumbing through it, not looking for anything in particular. I'd had my morning devotions earlier, though my time with God had not been particularly profitable. That day my appointment with God had been routine, just a custom not to be broken.

But as I thumbed through the Scripture, I glanced at Matthew 14 and stopped. I started to read about those disciples in the boat. They too were feeling alone when the waves were about to swamp them. They thought that Jesus was off in the hills somewhere conversing with his Father in prayer, certainly not thinking about them.

And it was true. Jesus was off praying. But the Scripture indicates that he saw them, he saw their need, and he came to them walking on the sea. In a few minutes a calm had come, and the disciples worshiped him. I realized that in all of their fear, in their feeling of being alone, though they didn't realize it then, Jesus knew exactly where they were and what was happening to them.

Then it hit me! Jesus knows where I am too. He understands my loneliness. He knows all about my depression. He understands how my emotions go up and down depending on my thoughts or my situation or the weather. He knows when I am far from my family and miss them. And this same Jesus who could calm the wild sea and give peace to those fishermen can handle my problems too.

I began to look at my situation with a new expectancy. How will he help me? How will he support me? My mind went back to the many times and situations when he had met me before. The waves had come before, and in those times when I thought that he didn't see me he *had* seen me and known of my loneliness.

And I thought: How can I tell that to the newly widowed who feel so alone and deserted by God? How can I tell that to the one in the hospital who has been awake all night thinking about what the doctors told him the day before? How can I convince the lonely student who cannot find a friend? And how can I tell those who have no family left: "Jesus knows where you are; he sees"?

Then, because God sometimes uses what is already in our minds, a passage of Scripture came to me. It was one I intended to preach on a few days later in a Japanese church. I had thought carefully about that passage because I would have an interpreter, and I wanted to be sure that I fully understood the text. Those words came into my mind as a comfort to me: "For the eyes of the Lord move to and fro throughout the earth that He may strongly support those whose heart is completely His" (2 Chron. 16:9, NASB).

And I knew that God was looking at me. He sees me. He always has, he always will.

God is smiling even when I'm all alone. And we are alone—sometimes even when we are in a crowd. But we don't have to be victims of loneliness; we can use what we have when we are all alone. Harold B. Walker said, "There is no escape from the truth that at the core of our minds we are profoundly alone. We have a choice, therefore, between loneliness and solitude, between melancholy and depression."

The ancient philosophers knew the value of the lone mind. For those thinkers, their minds were a laboratory. They worked with thought and often did it walking, perhaps as Plato did, through olive groves. God touches us, often in the deepest part of our being, when we are alone. We can think when we are alone. Indeed that's why those ancient philosophers often found themselves somewhat apart from society—for society then as now preferred the active, the noisy, the aggressive, the busy-ness that tranquilizes the mind and keeps it from working.

The human mind needs God, and often he comes to our minds with his deepest teaching when we are alone. He is the God of the mind as much as the will. We are instructed to be transformed by the renewing of our minds (Rom. 12:2). Alone we ponder, alone we can be creative, alone we can learn to express on paper or in art our inner discoveries. Man needs to be alone. For out of solitude comes clear thinking that helps him, and through loneliness can come growth.

Not everyone wants to be alone. Many grow into themselves when they are alone, almost narcotized by the sameness of their self-imposed confinement.

Harold B. Walker said, "The recluse is a sad and lonely man whose attitudes and feelings are distorted by his lack of companionship. His opinions have no source for correction and modification. His feelings fester without the healing grace of sharing. His ways are never challenged by the company of others. Lonely and depressed, he has no surcease from the self-pity that engulfs his life. His aloneness is no virtue if there is nothing in it beyond aloneness. . . .

"The empty mind turns inward and is bounded by the self. It is haunted by remembered hurts and anxious fears, swamped in the end by towering waves of self-pity. Its inscape is bleak and its horizons zero. The full mind turns outward to embrace the things of beauty that are a joy forever. . . .

"We cannot sweep our minds clear of self-pity, fear, anxiety, and loneliness unless we fill the vacuum with ideas and knowledge that crowd out the unwanted and the hurtful."

Except for this danger of growing inward, of listening only to self and not to God, being alone gives opportunity to do more, give more, expand more, think deeper, grow stronger, and this is missed by those who will not accept lonely times.

We need in our world the people, especially Christians, who grow when they are all alone. Those who know how to utilize the gifts of Christ in the alone times can be the innovators, the thinkers, and the teachers for the vast portion of society who won't be alone to think. For example, I know college graduates who haven't read a book (of any kind) since graduation twenty or thirty years before. Some don't even read a newspaper. They don't want to stretch or think. What if our world were left to them?

People who won't think must be cared for. They must be helped to think, to understand, to grasp both themselves and their world. Why? The answer is admittedly a Christian one: so that in understanding themselves and their world they will know how much they need God's wholeness. Only when he thinks will man turn to the Savior and come to live under the smile of God. The nonthinker, filling his life with noise and pulsing sensations, won't do it; neither will the nonactivist who goes inward with only himself as a resource.

Man must be shown God—the omnipotent yet all-present God. Man must be shown the Incarnate Son, the Emmanuel, the God with us. And only as he stops, thinks, and questions will he be open to this One who is other than himself.

If it weren't so painful, it could be amusing to hear the statements from people who won't think but have all the "answers" that discount God. Most of the time there is no explaining to them because there is no starting point of thought—not thought about philosophy or theology, that is unnecessary—but thought about their own experiences of life. Unless one will think, he will not respond. He needs to be helped to think. The quiet believer can do that. He has stopped outside the nonthinking environment that most live in, and has put together the thoughts that others can grasp, if they are willing.

Alone, we have time to pray and opportunity to receive God's biblical counsel. There is an example of this in Scripture: In 1 Chronicles 28:9 David spoke to his son Solomon. His words were given on the occasion of the building of the temple, but now his words teach anyone who seeks the wisdom of God as Solomon did. This is God's counsel; it is given through David, yes, and it is given to Solomon, but it is God's counsel without limit for all time. It is given to us. " 'Solomon, my son, get to know the God of your fathers. Worship and serve him with a clean heart and a willing mind, for the Lord sees every heart and understands and knows every thought. If you seek him, you will find him; but if you forsake him, he will permanently throw you aside. So, be very careful, for the Lord has chosen you to build his holy temple. Be strong and do as he commands.' " (1 Chron. 28:9-11, TLB). This is counsel for us.

If you have a lot of time alone, God knows and will use it. God knows if you are suddenly widowed, or if you lose your children, or if your friends move away or die, or you find yourself living alone for any reason; that is God's potential time—a gift. God isn't closing

128

shop on you. He will lead when you are alone. That is a special time for the personal and majestic touch of God.

When I was a seminary student in Philadelphia, I was working long hours to earn enough money to pay my tuition. I worked weekends in a church in New York and carried a full course load. I was so busy that I couldn't even get enough sleep. I certainly couldn't be alone with my thoughts and God. But one week I was sick. My parents telephoned me the day before I was to leave for my weekend in New York, and they could tell that I was sick. My dad offered to send me the wages I would have earned had I gone to my student ministry that weekend. Having that gift of money, I was able to telephone the church, tell them I was too sick to come, and stay in my room. It was my time with God—a retreat.

The building was quiet that weekend as other students were out on their ministry assignments. I slept, recuperated, studied, and I did a lot of thinking. It was then, in the quiet time—a luxury I hadn't had in several years—that I was able to think about my life and get a sense of direction.

I also found myself thinking about and then writing a letter to a girl in Chicago—a letter I hadn't had time to think about before. But I remember saying later to a friend, "I wrote a letter after a lot of prayer, and I feel such peace about it. I believe that she is the girl I'm going to marry." And the next year I did marry her.

God didn't cause me to be sick. But he used the quiet time to reach me as he hadn't been able to before. That isn't rationalism after the fact; I sensed him near me then. I knew I was having a special weekend with God. I had time with him. There is rest and healing in the quiet of being alone with God. Those are discerning times, influencing everything that we do.

In the Book of Numbers, a book of Scripture that is not often read, is a passage that tells a lot about life as God wants us to live it. "So it was that they camped or traveled at the commandment of the Lord; and whatever the Lord told Moses they should do, they did" (Num. 9:23, TLB).

At the command of the Lord they camped; at the command of the Lord they set out. Whether they stayed still or moved forward, they responded to the word of God. There is just as much obedience in standing still, in not acting, as there is in movement and action. We often forget that. We want to be moving out and going ahead all the time. But there is a time to stop and regroup, a time to stand still, a time to rest, to get organized and wait for God's next order. It is important for progress.

Christine Wood, an English writer, in her article in *Decision* magazine, July, 1981, taught that the tide cannot keep coming in; it has to go back before it can come again on the next wave. There is as much progress in retreat as there is in advance. No one can advance all of the time. We have to stand still, even go back, to gain a momentum for the next advance. We have to encamp if there is to be the strength to go on. We need our times alone; we need perspective, a withdrawal time, to get a better view of all that so often gives anxiety when we are in its midst.

Maybe that's why God gave one day a week for special rest. I like Sundays; I like the quiet time to think.

Worship, Sunday school, and evening service feed me. They bless me and bring me into a supportive prayer fellowship. Those hours in church focus my attention on God, who he is and what he does. But that still leaves quiet times on Sunday.

I don't work on Sunday, so I'm free to be quiet. It is a "down" time but a rich time. I wouldn't work on Sundays for anything if I could get out of it, or if I did have to work, I would have another day with no work just because I have the need for quiet time with God. I need a day when my mind isn't working on some project or anticipating the next day's work. Even if I doze off for a nap or turn on the television or read a book, I'm at rest. Because none of what I'm doing is "required," my mind is free, and in this freedom I have had some great times with God. He has taught me, led me, and encouraged me. I've found myself basking in the warmth of his smile.

God wants us to encamp as the children of Israel did, to listen to him, to get our orders, to renew our strength. Then we can move out again. There is a blessed rest, a quiet, in the presence of the One who gives us our orders. There is satisfaction in knowing that we are doing the right thing even when at the moment we are not doing anything, just sitting by the door of our tent.

I know a woman who is only happy when she is partying. She has to be with a crowd, she has to be going. She thinks being active, being involved, mixing it up all the time, is wonderful. But it's wearing her out, and it's a mark of her own insecurity. She doesn't know the Lord; she doesn't know the place of peace and rest, she can't enjoy her own company.

She's too busy trying to escape her own company. She does not know the great satisfaction that God offers: "Be still, and know that I am God" (Ps. 46:10, KJV).

We who are God's people, coming under his orders, advance when he commands and stay still when he commands. In quiet, alone, we hear the orders. We can think, we can put together the complicated parts of life, and then we can act and help others to act.

Being alone is not bad; it can be good—if our company is God's company. For when we live under and enjoy the smile of God, we aren't really alone at all.

E L E V E N
If I Should Die Before I Wake

The Christian faith is the answer to death because it is the answer to life.

I have in my files a clipping from *Christianity Today*, February 1, 1963, in which an 82-year-old pastor, the Reverend S. F. Marsh of Leland, Mississippi, talked about his own death. He said he had been getting ready for death for most of his life because fifty-five years earlier he had struggled with tuberculosis. Every year he expected to die. Apparently the fact that he was then eighty-two years of age surprised him. He said, "I have been getting ready for the last impressive hour for many, many years."

That's a delightful thought: "The last impressive hour." Everything Mr. Marsh did was in anticipation of and in preparation for that last impressive hour. Whether he was preaching, teaching, or caring for people, everything was weighed not by its greatness at the moment but by the belief that this might be his last message, his last act of kindness. Always he was getting ready for that last impressive hour.

If we, like the Reverend Mr. Marsh, always had our death before us, it would influence everything that we do. We would sit by the bedside of a sick child just as readily as calling on presidents, advising business leaders, or holding high office. Perspectives change and values are measured differently in the light of getting ready for that last impressive hour. Mr. Marsh went on to say, "In all these and a thousand other activities I was getting ready to die. Let me make a suggestion here. Just go along living a Christian life of usefulness the way a Christian should, and when you approach eighty-two you'll find yourself thinking, 'Why, I've been getting ready for my last hour on earth for a long time.' "

It is not a morbid thing to think about—getting ready for death. Quite the contrary, it makes every hour before it so much more meaningful. No wonder the Apostle Paul could say that he was willing to leave the body and be present with the Lord (2 Cor. 5:8). Why not? He had an ongoing work that was measured in the light of eternity. If it went on another year, then he would have another year's ministry. If it ended that day, he'd be present with the Lord. It didn't matter. What a wonderful balance for thinking about life.

Most people, even Christians, fear death—at least they fear the dying process. Then there are other Christians who make death sound like such a delightful thing that they doubt the Christian faith of any who fear it. They become spiritually superior— looking down their noses at those who tremble at the unknown, the passage into heaven. We may fear the pain of death, the sickness that brings on the deterioration of the body, the anxiety. We do fear what we have never experienced before. We don't know what dying will be like. There is nothing un-Christian in being concerned about the process of dying.

We Christians are entitled to depression. We are weak—that's why we need the Strong One. We are finite—that's why we need the Infinite. When a Christian talks about being free from the fear of death, he is really talking about not being afraid of meeting God.

The Christian is God's child through adoption. The Bible says, "And so we should not be like cringing, fearful slaves, but we should behave like God's very own children, adopted into the bosom of his family, and calling to him, 'Father, Father'" (Rom. 8:15, TLB).

But being human, we still have instincts for self-preservation. I don't want to be run over by a car. I don't want to be burned in a nuclear blast. I don't want to have a hideous cancer or go blind. I don't want that.

But I know God and I know that some day I "... shall be like him; for [I] shall see him as he is" (1 John 3:2, KJV). Therefore, as I prepare for death I am both happy and sad. Fortunately the desire for liberation from all the pain of this earth grows as that last day on earth approaches so that even the deterioration and pain that may lead to death does not seem as frightening.

If our life here has been good because we have drawn on the gifts, the promises, the love, the wisdom of God, and have lived in him, how much more then is waiting for us when we move out beyond the limitations of this world? Don't be afraid to say "goodbye" to this world and walk out of it with him.

What do you think death is? Do you realize that you have no idea at all what death is? You have not experienced it, nor have you talked with anyone who has. We read books about those returning from a death state. We are eager to know what they were feeling, to record what they tell. We want to know.

Some say they were happy and experienced a sense of light and peace. Others were frightened, terror-stricken. But these reports are only that—reports. We don't know where these "dead" people were, or even if they were dead at all—we still don't know the meaning of death. The Christian does know, on the authority of God's Word, that when Christ appears "we will be like him" (1 John 3:2, KJV).

The fear of annihilation, the end of us, is not a legitimate fear for one who is alive in Christ. For the Christian has already been through real death. He now faces only physical death; that is not annihilation, it is liberation. Even the process, the journey, can be an experience with God. We can look forward to the journey for even if it is through a valley, he is with us in that journey (Ps. 23:4).

And when the journey is over, when we are "gone," will that produce sorrow in those around us? Of course it will. Jesus felt sorrow for Lazarus (John 11:33–35). Our friends, our relatives, are bound to be hurt by our cessation of life. They will miss us. That's normal, that's healthy; but it also makes the anticipation of reunion with one another much sweeter.

One of the important things about anticipating our own death is that we likewise anticipate the deaths of others, and this influences the way we behave toward them. Don't leave yourself open to remorse and regret when you stand by a grave: "I should have treated him better." "Why didn't I do more?" "I should have shown more love." "We should have taken that trip together." "I should have listened to him." Know on the basis of your own mortality the mortality of others, and leave people in a way that will deposit for you and them good memories no matter who goes first.

In Christ, death and hell have been judged. In Christ there is new birth, a beginning. We move not toward the end of life. We are moving toward a fuller life in all of its completion and fulfillment. We work and act not to become something—we already *are* something. It is already clear where we are going, and we move toward the excitement of that. The progression we enjoy is our own further growing in him. This is not life after life, this is life itself. This is not a great cyclical development leading to the Hindu liberation, it is a moving from the very point where human religions will never be. We are going from new birth in Christ —a post-grave life—into life developing in Christ.

Ludwig Wittgenstein said, "Death is not an event in life. Death is not lived through."

But the Christian does live through it. Because he is already in the One who lived through it. For the unbeliever it is not so. The unbeliever only exists, he doesn't live. He doesn't live through death because he isn't even alive on this side of death. He goes on as he is now—existing as a created being but not as a living soul. He exists first on this side of death, then on the other, but apart from God. That is his choice. He isn't the victim of fate or of some cruel cosmic roll of the dice; he has looked at the One who said, "I am come that they might have life" (John 10:10, KJV), and he has said no!

But, people ask, "How can one be moving and acting in this world and not be alive?" Doctors in a hospital decide when somebody is brain-dead even though his body is functioning. Is he alive? Likewise, if a person eats and works and sleeps but his soul is so hardened that he is not responding to the stimulus of God, is he alive? Activity is not the same as life. Commenting on Wittgenstein's quote, I wrote in *Decision* magazine:

> Ludwig Wittgenstein in his "tractatus Logico-Philosophicus" told his readers that death is not an event in life because it is not lived through. Now, that is something to think about. For the unsure person, that statement is frightening. For the Christian, that statement is erroneous.
>
> Jesus Christ is Victor over sin and death. In him, being redeemed, given new life, I have already been through death. Eternal life began for me the moment that I was born into that new life. My body will someday physically die, to be sure, and it will be buried. But let there be no mourning. Because I had eternal life from the moment of my new birth, I will keep right on going into an even fuller life, one without the encumbrances of the physical. I will go on with the eternal Christ. That is a surety for the Christian, because it isn't built on fantasy but on true hope, and that true hope, unlike wishful thinking, is certain.
>
> To the unsure person, Wittgenstein's statement is frightening because all that is beyond the body's cessation of function is unknown. Yet he has a sense that there is more; he has an innate awareness of the tripartite aspect of the human—the body, the mind, the spirit. What happens to that,

he wonders. He can't be sure and assumes that no one else can be sure either.

God, in Christ, acted upon the separation and death that mankind brought upon himself by his own volition. Because God has acted, man doesn't have to have eternal death; he chooses to die by refusing God's gift of new life in Jesus Christ. He can choose that life, he doesn't have to go cursing and screaming into death as so many do when the reality of death hits them. He doesn't have to be always unsure, trying to forget what his mind won't let him forget. He doesn't have to pretend that all is well by gathering like-minded people around him who by unspoken agreement keep each other busy lest they face a moment of doubt about what will happen when their self-generated party is over.

With the believers of the ages, we can and do rejoice in the risen Christ. Raised with him, we shout our Hallelujahs! Jesus Christ lives. We can say with the apostle, "Death is swallowed up in victory. O death, where is thy sting? O grave, where is thy victory?" (1 Corinthians 15:54-55, KJV).

We can live right past Easter into the fullest life, whether it is here in time or there in eternity. Death and its root of sin are conquered; it is settled for us; we are alive forever—and it is life as it was intended to be.

For it is always true of the one who has responded to the proffered gift of life: "I am crucified with Christ: nevertheless I live; yet not I, but Christ liveth in me; and the life which I now live in the flesh I live by the faith of the Son of God, who loved me, and gave himself for me" (Galatians 2:20, KJV).

If there ever is a nonevent for the Christian, it is his own death. He has already been through real death—with the Conqueror.

How sad then that we talk of growing old in the same way as the world does. We are not moving toward death but from death toward greater and greater life. For we are dead in Christ now and alive in Christ now. The life that has already been to the grave and hell is our life, and in him we have come out on the other side with heaven before us. Life in its fullness is the life within us, to be even so much richer when the encumbrances of the dead world that hold us drop away. How good, then, to be reaching toward next year or the next decade! How we can rejoice in each passing year and dedicate the years remaining to using every moment faithfully for the One who takes us by the hand and leads us and calls us his own. How good to "offer [our] bodies as living sacrifices, holy and pleasing to God—which is [our] spiritual worship" (Rom. 12:1, NIV). How good then, not to be conformed to the world but to be "transformed by the renewing of [our] mind[s]. Then [we] will be able to test and approve what God's will is—his good, pleasing and perfect will" (Rom. 12:2, NIV). We are in the process of living, and someday we will be more alive than we are now.

And so we enter into rest. A holy rest. It is not a rest of sitting around bored, neither here now nor in heaven later. It is a rest of completion, a rest of accomplishment. For we have all of that in him who is complete even as we continue to move along on this earth, serving, loving, giving, and obeying. We rest in the security of knowing to whom we belong, where we have come from and where we are going. We have the rest of knowing that even our work is not our accomplishment whether or not it is completed by our definition of complete. Ours is the rest of knowing that he is Lord, he is the One in control—the God of history, the Master of our lives. Ours is the rest of knowing that we belong to the eternal God who is in all yet above all and beyond all. He is our rest, our true security.

We belong now in the physical creation as God's created ones, and we belong outside creation as the redeemed children of our heavenly Father. We are citizens of both time and eternity. We are not finishing our lives, we are just beginning our lives—for we have him, his very gift of life, and we will have that for all eternity. This security is God's love gift to us, his great heart gift—and it is intended for all. Some will miss it. That is the saddest of all realities. But others will find it, and in that we continually rejoice.

People tease: "You're not getting older, you are getting better." They may only be joking about it, but for the Christian that is true. And because it is true and we know it, we can handle whatever comes to us on this journey we call life. And we can handle our death.

Who is going to manage your death? Think about that now before you are incapacitated. Do you want heroic methods used to prolong your life? I've known cancer patients who, although given no hope, still allowed their lives to be prolonged only a few weeks with great pain and sickness. It isn't that the treatments might have worked; the doctors and the patients knew that they wouldn't because of the nature of the disease. This isn't an argument for euthanasia, terminating everyone who "ceases to be useful"—not at all. Life is too precious. It is a gift from God. But it is a question of the dignity of personal choice—especially for the Christian who is going home.

Arrange with your family now about who is going to make decisions when you are dying. Personally, I don't want to undo a lifetime of trying to be an encouragement and help to others by becoming a financial and an emotional strain on everyone during my last weeks. I'd like the dignity of loving and giving even in my death.

But I don't say that out of fear of prolonged personal suffering. Suffering personally is different from inflicting suffering on others. We can suffer and endure it, even teach the dignity and the strength of suffering as we go through it. But allowing ourselves to die may be the better gift to those left behind. Each of us needs to think that through.

There is always another side to suffering, especially for the Christian. I've been thinking about the story of Margaret of Molokai. "Forty-seven years ago a twelve-year-old girl was taken from a hula recital in the city hall to exile on the island of Molokai. Over these years, she lost three husbands to leprosy. Her four children were taken from her at birth and delivered to adoptive families on the mainland. Over the years, the disease mangled her feet and hands."

What did she say about this? "I no blame God for

disease. I blame germs. . . . If my pain no get better, I become one better person from my pain."

Is there value in suffering? Obviously there is. It can make us and those around us rethink our human frailty, our dependence upon family, our need for God. God is not sadistic when he allows us to suffer. There is teaching in suffering, for us and for others. Don't be afraid of suffering; it is an enemy, but it is not greater than God's grace. Use pain—let it teach you about yourself, your strengths, your resolves, your commitment. You can grow too, through the value of your pain-free minutes and the gift of yourself to others.

Years ago I read *The Man Who Lived Twice*. I never forgot that book. Edward Sheldon, a Broadway actor, was crippled by arthritis. He spent his remaining years blind and unable to move. Yet from his bed he touched the lives of great numbers of people with his encouragement and help. He was a giving man.

There may be great pain ahead for some of us in this life, or there may not. But there will be death. Don't be afraid to think about death while you are still strong and in the full bloom of life. You needn't fear it. Be ready for it.

If you are killed accidentally, have you already arranged your will to take care of your family? Have you already arranged for useful body parts to be given to somebody else so that he can live? As a Christian, if you would work day and night for the salvation of a soul, won't you also donate what you can no longer use for the benefit of someone else's life? If someone is starving, would you feed him? If he needs an eye or a kidney, will you provide it?

As you think about death, not morbidly, not in a ghoulish fashion but as an inevitable part of the experience of living, see it as an adventure. It is the next step, the graduation, the translation, the moving out of here and into there. To anticipate death makes all of life fall into perspective. What you do now counts. The time you waste now counts too. And the mistakes that you make now, in the long run, don't really matter. Nor do the successes.

Don't be surprised when death comes. Be ready for it, excited about it. Be secure in the anticipation of it.

One Sunday afternoon when Jimmy Carter was President of the United States, Andrea and I were invited to the White House for an afternoon with the Carters and other guests, mostly people related to Christian media. It was an informal time in the "backyard" of the White House. At breakfast that morning I thought, "This afternoon I'll picnic at the White House with the President." And later we did, enjoying the music and informal conversation with President and Mrs. Carter under the warm summer sun.

That made me think past that particular afternoon to a future event. There will come a day, whether I'm in a hospital bed or at home, when I'll be able to say, "This evening I'll banquet with the Lord in his House."

That thought went through my mind again three years later, this time at lunch with President Reagan. Only something else was added. I looked around and thought, "The White House is the same, but the Presidents change." Someday I'll be in God's mansion where there is a room prepared for me, and the Host will never move out. He who invites us to heaven will always be there. No matter what changes now, God does not change ever—nor does my place with him. "But thou art the same, and thy years shall have no end. The children of thy servants shall continue, and their seed shall be established before thee" (Ps. 102:27, 28, KJV). I'm going to live with God!

I want to be ready for that so when I arrive and circulate among friends and visit with God and listen to the music and enjoy the warm sunshine, I'll be able to say, "I'm glad I was invited. I'm glad I'm here."

Death is total gain; we must never forget that. "For to me, living means opportunities for Christ, and dying—well, that's better yet!" (Phil. 1:21, TLB).

The death of a Christian is precious to God. "His loved ones are very precious to him and he does not lightly let them die" (Ps. 116:15, TLB).

Don't worry about the suffering of those who have gone on before you. Or even about all that happened leading to their deaths. Whether it was torture or other pain, they are past it now; God is already wiping away their tears. "And God shall wipe away all tears from their eyes" (Rev. 21:4, KJV).

No death is a surprise to God. He is prepared for our death even if it surprises us. He knows exactly when it will occur, and he is ready. It will come right on time. He is there at your death, beside you.

The Psalmist expressed, "Thou art with me; thy rod and thy staff they comfort me" (Ps. 23:4, KJV).

Death is both a final act and a prelude, for we are living sacrifices. Death is part of our worship. Death—that final sacrifice—is the last drop of this libation given in our worship. Then the fight here will have been fought, the last gift to God complete. Now there is nothing more to offer. Now for us is a face-to-face enjoyment—forever.

Thomas à Kempis said, "For he that loveth God with all his heart dreadeth neither death nor punishment, nor judgment, nor Hell; for perfect love giveth sure access to God."

We will at last be the perfection that God intended. Think of having a nature that is no longer rebellious but which responds to God easily and naturally. "We shall be like him; for we shall see him as he is" (1 John 3:2, KJV).

Like him! What a holy wonder that will be!

And, of course, the last word on the matter of death is God's Word. "There shall be no more death" (Rev. 21:4, KJV). "Death is swallowed up in victory" (1 Cor. 15:54, KJV).

Victory! It is ours, in the risen Christ now; it is ours in the risen Christ then. He is our proof that truly we live, and live, and live forever, under the smile of God.

TWELVE
Enjoying the Smile of God

Alone in a hotel restaurant in Nagoya, Japan, I sat watching the fish swimming in a little stream outside the dining room window. The Japanese, in an artistic, creative way, often surround a hotel with plantings and streams. It gives a pastoral feeling even when the hotel is situated in the midst of factories and commercial buildings.

One hotel in Tokyo has gardens and streams placed in a tiny area, giving a feeling of spaciousness. An Osaka hotel has a waterfall, creating the appearance of a deep forest even though directly behind the waterfall, out of sight, is an ugly factory. The stream from the waterfall flows down through greenery, right into the lounge of the hotel.

But there in Nagoya, I watched the fish. They were all colors. Some were red, some blue, some gold, some green, and some were even mottled, having many colors. They swam leisurely, and as I sat watching them I sensed a calm come over me. They gave a comforting mental change from the worries of a hectic day. They were beautiful fish—but they were carp!

How can scavenger fish like carp be beautiful? These were. I had always thought that if I had to be a fish I would want to be a rainbow trout or something tropical and exotic. But there they were, ordinary carp to whom God had given beautiful colors to make them esthetically pleasing to watch.

Most of us are ordinary too—like carp. Yet just as God can take an ordinary carp and give it the beautiful hues of tropical fish, he can do the same with us.

I may be just a carp, but I can be beautiful to watch. Maybe I'm just a carp, but I can bring something uplifting into drab lives. I may not be an "exotic species," but I can have an influence on people even if all I ever do is "swim" by.

God made me. To many I may seem to be an ordinary piece of creation, but I'm not. There is beauty in me because God put it there.

A Christian may be "ordinary" or live in plain or even ugly settings, but by the touch of God he can be beautiful to all who are around him. That beauty, even in its silent passing near by, brings peace. It gives people the hope that "maybe God can do something beautiful in me too."

In Nagoya, the fish swam quietly. But their influence gave me a different perspective on my surroundings and my day. If God can do that with a carp for me, what can he do with me for others?

I want to be a beautiful carp even if all I ever do is swim by for someone to see. A carp can point to the beauty of God, and give peace. I want to do that too. And I know I can as I live under, and live enjoying, the wonderful smile of God.

God loves you. You know that he does. Let him do what he wants to do in your life; let him express that love for you. Isn't it time you started living every day —with good times and the bad—under the smile of God? Isn't it time?

In Exodus 23:20 God said, "Behold, I send an Angel before thee, to keep thee in the way, and to bring thee into the place which I have prepared" (KJV).

Here is a promise that none of us can ignore. This is God's Word to his own people. He will guard us; he will bring us into the place which he has prepared. There is an assurance here of the leadership of God. He will do with us and for us what we cannot do for ourselves. We could never adequately guard ourselves. Not on the streets, not in the world, not in our relationships to other people. But God has sent his angels, his ministering angels, to help us. "He shall give his angels charge over thee" (Ps. 91:11, KJV).

He provides the protection for us and he has a place for us. We don't have to run around seeking God's protection or agonize if we don't see the angels who are around us. We have one responsibility, to be obedient to the One who sends his angels. God guards me; my responsibility is not to be disobedient or rebellious. God's Word promises that he will guard me and lead me into the place he has prepared for me—even if I am "only" a carp.

In surrender, in the refusal to be rebellious, is the key to the door of God's caring love. In Numbers 1:54 we read: "So all these instructions of the Lord to Moses were put into effect" (TLB).

These sons of Israel did exactly what God told them to do; they obeyed every order given by God. He could lead them because he knew that they would carry out his orders.

Did they understand every command that God gave? Probably not. Did they know the outcome of every order? They couldn't possibly have known.

They had one objective—to obey. God gave them orders; they did what he said.

We have our orders too. God knows what he is doing with us. He knows the thoughts he thinks toward us (Jer. 29:11). He has an expected end for us; he loves us with an everlasting love. Our job is to obey him.

H. C. G. Moule said, "Let my mental habit be so full of 'my Master,' that I shall be on the watch, always and everywhere, to be used by Him, or to 'stand and wait' close to Him, as He pleases; only always knowing myself to be His property, and glad indeed so to be."

There is freedom in that obedience, great freedom. We don't struggle anymore. We walk, we run, we act —on his terms, by his orders, for his sake. And we know as we do it that we are his. Jesus put it in terms that we can all understand: "Ye are my friends, if ye do whatsoever I command you" (John 15:14, KJV). Friends, obedient friends—and more than that, we are heirs of God and joint heirs with Christ. As heirs we are to obey. Let there be for all of us heirs life in fullness, a life under the smile of God.

David said, " . . . you love me! You are holding my right hand! You will keep on guiding me all my life with your wisdom and counsel; and afterwards receive me into the glories of heaven! Whom have I in heaven but you? And I desire no one on earth as much as you! My health fails; my spirits droop, yet God remains! He is the strength of my heart; he is mine forever!

"But those refusing to worship God will perish, for he destroys those serving other gods.

"But as for me, I get as close to him as I can! I have

chosen him and I will tell everyone about the wonderful ways he rescues me" (Ps. 73:23-28, TLB).

Jesus, by a miracle, provided a large catch of fish for his disciples. But they had to obey his command to draw it in. They even had to obey him when he told them where to cast their net. They did obey, and look what Jesus did! He invited them to haul in and cook their fish, yet he was the one who provided that meal.

Life is that way. When we obey him, he tells us where to cast the net. He gives to us abundantly, often more than we could ever ask. Our nets nearly break with his goodness. And he gives us the meal to share in, too. He does that for all of us. That biblical illustration of the fish tells far more than the story of one miracle; that illustration tells of the great care and concern God provides by helping us to do what we already know how to do. These men were all fishermen —not successful that night, but they were all fishermen. They knew how to cast nets, they knew how to haul in the fish, they knew what to do with the fish they caught. But Jesus provided for the fishermen in all their circumstances in a way that they understood best—he provided lots of fish.

God does that for us. He provides for us in our circumstances in a way that we understand best. Sometimes we look for the unusual while he provides his miracle in ordinary ways. As he did for these professional fishermen, he gives us the same provision every day; it comes because he makes it happen. And again, as he did for the disciples on the shore, in the meal that he provides he may give not a banquet but a few fish. The point is, he does it. When we see the substance of life like that under the guidance of his hand, we begin to understand the daily miracle of living with him and we have cause for daily thanksgiving. Martyn Lloyd-Jones said, "It is God Himself who gives us life, and the body in which we live it; and if He has done that we can draw this deduction, that His purpose with respect to us will be fulfilled. God never leaves unfinished any work He will most surely fulfill. And therefore we come back to this, that there is a plan for every life in the mind of God."

As I write this, it is Saturday morning. I woke early. In fact, it is 2:30 A.M. Why I woke now, I don't know. I thought about some deadlines that were pushing at me. I couldn't touch them anyway until I made some long distance calls on Monday morning. I thought about a lot of other things, as we all do when we can't sleep.

Finally I got up and came down here to my base-ment-study to work on this final chapter. The things I had written before haunted me. I wondered, am I a hypocrite to write about living under the smile of God when I wake up at 2:30 A.M.? Am I one who worries just as those who do not have a heavenly Father to trust? I thought about failure, frustration, the lack of what I'd like to see accomplished in my life, and I wondered about me, about God, about his smile.

Then I reread the opening story in this chapter and thought about carp, and me, and the blemishes on what God would like to make beautiful. My mind began to wander as I thought about another event in another Japanese city and what it taught me about myself. I had unintentionally embarrassed a gentle Japanese floor manager in an Osaka hotel. I was standing outside his office on the fourteenth floor of the hotel waiting for an appointment when I noticed a beautiful flowering plant on a desk. So I walked over to admire it and said, "It is very pretty." The manager looked at me, then at the plant, and suddenly his eyes showed alarm for he saw what I had not seen. There was a dead leaf on the stem.

He was embarrassed. Quickly he stripped off the dead leaf and moved the plant behind a lamp. By his words, which I did not understand, and his action, which I did understand, he was showing that he was ashamed. He was conscious that I had seen less than his best. His plant had a dead leaf on it. And all I could do, as I realized what he was thinking, was to back away and repeat, "It is a very pretty plant."

We bring shame to people in so many ways. Often it is without any intention of ever doing so. Yet their embarrassment is not something that we can control; it is in that other person's mind. The other person is seeing or feeling something that we do not perceive. If only I could have told that quiet, gentle man that I was not drawing attention to a fault, that I really did admire his plant.

Sometimes we are ashamed ourselves by something that another person says to us, not because he wants to shame us but because the feeling of shame is already harbored inside. If someone expresses what he thinks is an innocent thought or observation about me, sometimes I am ashamed. For I know that there are "dead leaves" in my life. Knowing that can mar my attitude, the way I speak, and can even make me avoid others. It can mar my witness too; I hide for shame that someone will see my "dead leaf."

And yet one dead leaf doesn't mar the beauty of a

whole plant. Neither does error, real or imagined, destroy the beauty of a believer. It is important that any flaw be taken away, for it is a shameful thing to see the "dead leaves" in our lives and leave them there. But there is no cause for shame if we want to get rid of them and do. When we go to God about "that leaf," he trims the plant and removes the shame. That's the kind of considerate gardener he is.

God sees the overall beauty of the believer in Christ. If flaws are there, they are not a reason for hiding or withdrawal. The flaws are to be stripped away, but the flower, the beauty of the believer, can still be displayed.

Zephaniah the prophet said, "The unjust knoweth no shame" (Zeph. 3:5, KJV)—and that's true. But the Christian is not "unjust." The Christian is one who has been made just in Jesus Christ. That's why Christians feel shame when unbelievers often do not. Because the Christian knows the beauty of holiness, he knows when he has strayed from it. The unjust does not know holiness, does not know that he himself is marred. He feels no shame.

Shame has value if it is allowed to have its improving work in the life of a believer. It comes not to make him withdraw or feel embarrassed, it comes to remind him of his greater beauty in Christ, a beauty not in himself but a beauty of holiness that needs to be displayed because "it is no longer I who live, but Christ lives in me" (Gal. 2:20, NASB). That "Christ in me" life is not to be hidden by shame.

This morning, in this quiet house, with the rest of the family asleep, as I pray there are thoughts I have to put into action. I must as a Christian be quick to strip off the dead leaves, but I can't as a Christian think that dead leaves destroy the beauty of the plant. A beautiful plant is still that, even with an occasional untrimmed, unsightly, and somewhat distracting dead leaf. As a believer I can and must display the true beauty that is placed in me, allowing the Gardener to find and trim what is unsightly and dead.

The beauty of a believer is never in himself; it is in the work of God. We show his beauty as he opens up the flower in us. We neither hide our beauty nor assume that we can promote it as our own. It is not ours because we are not our own.

The plant on that man's desk in Osaka should not have been hidden behind a lamp. Once he trimmed the dead leaf he should have pushed that plant forward for me to see. He hid it, but he didn't have to. He was ashamed, but he shouldn't have been.

We don't have to be ashamed either. Just as that floor manager identified the ugly part of his plant and got rid of it, so day by day the same must be true in my life and yours. Why should any dead part mar the beauty of God's plant? God made us and set us out for the world to see. Beautiful and on display, the Christian needs to be seen. God is not ashamed of the beauty he gives us. We are not to be either. God plants, trims, waters, tenderly encourages and, most of all, provides the warmth of his smile. We can live under that warm, life-giving smile of God. It is the only place where we can provide beauty for the world to see. In a not very pretty world, God has in us something to show.

Be what God made you to be—live under the smile of God.